Cruise Missile Proliferation in the 1990s

THE WASHINGTON PAPERS

... intended to meet the need for an authoritative, yet prompt, public appraisal of the major developments in world affairs.

President, CSIS: David M. Abshire

Series Editor: Walter Laqueur

Director of Publications: Nancy B. Eddy

Managing Editor: Donna R. Spitler

MANUSCRIPT SUBMISSION

The Washington Papers and Praeger Publishers welcome inquiries concerning manuscript submissions. Please include with your inquiry a curriculum vitae, synopsis, table of contents, and estimated manuscript length. Manuscript length must fall between 120 and 200 double-spaced typed pages. All submissions will be peer reviewed. Submissions to *The Washington Papers* should be sent to *The Washington Papers*; The Center for Strategic and International Studies; 1800 K Street NW; Suite 400; Washington, DC 20006. Book proposals should be sent to Praeger Publishers; 90 Post Road West; P.O. Box 5007; Westport, CT 06881.

Cruise Missile Proliferation in the 1990s

W. Seth Carus

Foreword by Janne E. Nolan

Published with the Center for
Strategic and International Studies
Washington, D.C.

PRAEGER

Westport, Connecticut
London

Library of Congress Cataloging-in-Publication Data

Carus, W. Seth.
  Cruise missile proliferation in the 1990s / W. Seth Carus.
     p.   cm. — (The Washington papers ; 159)
  "Published with the Center for Strategic and International
Studies, Washington, D.C."
  Includes bibliographical references and index.
  ISBN 0-275-94519-7 (HB). — ISBN 0-275-94520-0 (PB)
  1. Cruise missiles.   2. Arms control.   I. Center for Strategic
and International Studies (Washington, D.C.)   II. Title.
III. Series.
  UG1312.C7C37   1992   92-26115
  358.1'754—dc20

British Library Cataloging-in-Publication data is available.

Library of Congress Catalog Card Number: 92-26115
ISBN: 0-275-94519-7 (cloth)
        0-275-94520-0 (paper)

First published in 1992

Praeger Publishers, 88 Post Road West, Westport, CT 06881
An imprint of Greenwood Publishing Group, Inc.

Printed in the United States of America

∞™   1000125938

The paper used in this book complies with the Permanent
Paper Standard issued by the National Information Standards
Organization (Z39.48-1984).

10 9 8 7 6 5 4 3 2 1

Contents

Foreword

A steady trend for several decades, the proliferation of advanced weapons to volatile regions of the world seemed to come of age as an issue in the early 1990s. Partly this was the result of more focused attention by world leaders previously blinded by the preoccupations of superpower rivalry. In a highly stratified international security system divided between the technologically powerful few and a far weaker majority, it was long assumed that no Third World country could ever pose a serious threat to the great powers. With the exception of nuclear forces, efforts to control the international dissemination of weapons and technology were accordingly not given urgent priority.

The 1980s changed this perception. It was a time in which defense industries in the West and the former Soviet Union, under increasing fiscal constraints, competed for exports to almost any nation that could pay; when Third World weapons producers, such as China, North Korea, and Pakistan, were acquiring greater capabilities to develop and export weapons without interference from the industrial world or international law; when it was no longer possible to ignore the weaknesses of export controls, as Iraq, North Korea, and other military antagonists openly circumvented international strictures; and when the long-held illusion that Third World states could never pose a serious military threat to the United States or its allies was left to languish in the sands of the Iraqi desert.

The international community confronted a dramatic example of its failures to monitor and control the traffic in weapons of mass destruction in Iraq. Iraq's massive defense industrial base, which could develop, modify, and produce a wide range of unconventional military capabilities, demonstrated the consequences of a laissez-faire approach to global military commerce. Following the Iraqi invasion of Kuwait in August 1990, which precipitated the U.S.-led response in January 1991, every industrial country participating in the military coalition faced down weapons or technology that it had previously provided to Iraq—from Soviet SCUD missiles, to French Mirage aircraft, to the threat of German chemical materials believed to have found their way into Iraqi chemical artillery shells and ballistic missile warheads.

Coinciding with the trend toward a redistribution of military capabilities to developing countries and the ascendance of aggressive ambitions among a number of increasingly independent states, access to a new kind of weapon—cruise missiles—could alter military balances dramatically. With technology that is accessible, affordable, and relatively easy to produce, Third World countries could acquire highly accurate, long-range cruise missile forces to escalate local conflicts and threaten the forces or even the territories of the industrial powers. In this context, the tendency of the international community to ignore impending security threats until a crisis occurs is particularly ill-advised.

As those familiar with the work of Seth Carus have come to expect, the ensuing analysis of this emerging security threat is prescient, thorough, and original. Carus highlights a dimension of technology diffusion that has yet to capture sufficient attention from policymakers, but that could severely compound current security dilemmas. In this balanced and comprehensive account, Carus provides detailed analysis of how cruise missile technologies are acquired, produced, and deployed, as well as the likely military consequences. He also provides a prism through which to examine the broader challenge posed by a changing and increasingly porous international technology market.

This book is a warning to policymakers. It is not yet too late to confront the realities of cruise missile proliferation and to devise international responses that could at least contain its most adverse consequences. A new regime of technology controls, confidence- and security-building measures, and conflict resolution is needed. In addition to cruise missiles, there are other new technologies potentially even more dangerous to international stability, including antisatellite systems, or precision-strike munitions with deadly accuracies. Carus provides sensible policy recommendations. These should be heeded, without delay.

Janne E. Nolan
Senior Fellow
Brookings Institution

September 1992

Acknowledgments

Many people helped make this study possible, some of whom cannot be acknowledged publicly. Dr. Stephen Rosen of Harvard University is owed special thanks for organizing a John M. Olin Fellowship provided by the Naval War College Foundation. My interest in cruise missile proliferation owes much to Dr. James Roche, who also encouraged me to undertake this project. Stephen Glick provided able research and editorial support during the hectic final stages. Others who assisted me include Joseph S. Bermudez, Jr., Stephen Colwell of the Global Positioning Satellite Association, David C. Isby, Brad Roberts, and Steven J. Zaloga. I particularly thank George Lewis, who reviewed the draft manuscript for the Center for Strategic and International Studies (CSIS) and offered much constructive criticism.

Most of the research was conducted while I was at the Naval War College in Newport, Rhode Island. I am deeply grateful for the hospitality provided, especially by the library staff, and for the support of the John M. Olin and Naval War College foundations. I also thank CSIS for research funding that enabled me to finish the study.

The manuscript was completed in July 1991, while I was an employee of the Washington Institute for Near East Policy.

About the Author

W. Seth Carus completed this volume while a research fellow at the Washington Institute for Near East Policy. His most recently published works include *The Poor Man's Atomic Bomb? Biological Weapons in the Middle East*, a policy paper published by the Washington Institute, and *Ballistic Missiles in the Third World: Threat and Response*, a Washington Paper of the Center for Strategic and International Studies. During 1989–1990 he was an Olin Fellow at the Naval War College Foundation in Newport, Rhode Island. While at the Foundation, he wrote several articles on missile proliferation, including a study of the Iraqi missile program. Works written for the Washington Institute include *The Future Battlefield and the Arab-Israeli Conflict*, a book coauthored with Hirsh Goodman, "The Genie Unleashed: Iraqi Chemical and Biological Weapons," "Chemical Weapons in the Middle East," and "Missiles in the Middle East: A New Threat to Stability?" Seth Carus received a Ph.D. in international relations in 1987 from Johns Hopkins University.

Summary

During the past few years, there has been growing awareness of the potential dangers posed by the unchecked proliferation of surface-to-surface missiles. Until recently, attention focused primarily on the spread of ballistic missiles – a natural emphasis given the extensive use of ballistic missiles by Iraq during the 1991 Persian Gulf War. There is reason to believe, however, that during the 1990s a growing number of countries will concentrate their efforts on developing cruise missiles to supplement or even supplant ballistic missile programs.

The growing attractiveness of cruise missile technology results from the specific characteristics of such weapons and the growing availability of the technologies needed to produce them. Cruise missiles are well suited to delivery of chemical and biological agents, and, as demonstrated by the cruise missiles employed by the United States during the Gulf War, even conventionally armed systems can be highly effective if sufficiently accurate. This emphasizes the importance of the revolution in navigation technology. With readily accessible guidance technology, especially satellite navigation systems, it has become much easier to develop cruise missiles considerably more accurate than ballistic missiles of comparable range. Moreover, as discussed in some detail in this study, proliferating countries may be able to build cruise missiles with accuracies of 10 to 20 meters, and possibly less.

Many of the other technologies needed to produce cruise missiles are also becoming more widely available. Many developing countries have acquired antiship cruise missiles and remotely piloted vehicles, which are both systems that use technologies identical to those needed to produce cruise missiles. Indeed, there is significant evidence that a growing number of Third World countries are capable of producing airframes, engines, warheads, and guidance systems for cruise missiles.

Considerable efforts have been made to prevent the uncontrolled spread of cruise missile systems. The Missile Technology Control Regime, which was negotiated in 1987, recognized the potential threat posed by the proliferation of cruise missiles and provides a multilateral framework intended to inhibit efforts to acquire such weapons or the components and technology needed to make them.

The technology needed to produce cruise missiles is extensively available, however, and export controls can slow but not prevent their proliferation. Diplomatic pressure and arms control initiatives will also be needed, but the long-term prospects for such efforts are uncertain at best. As the decade proceeds, it will thus become increasingly important to ensure that the military forces of the United States and its allies have the defenses needed to defeat cruise missiles.

1

Introduction

Early on the morning of January 17, 1991, the U.S. Navy began launching Tomahawk tactical land attack missiles (TLAMs) at targets in Iraq. During the next two weeks, 288 of these cruise missiles were fired at high-priority targets, including sites located in the heart of Baghdad. Pentagon sources claimed that the missiles had an 85 percent success rate. During the same period, U.S. Navy strike aircraft launched seven standoff land attack missiles (SLAMs); this cruise missile was so new that it had not yet completed operational testing.[1]

The apparent success of these missiles appears to have vindicated the enthusiasm for land attack cruise missiles that led to the development of third-generation cruise missiles in the early 1970s. In contrast to the first-generation weapons, such as the German V-1 employed during World War II and the largely unsuccessful second-generation weapons developed starting in the late 1940s, the new missiles were highly accurate and reliable. It was not until the 1991 Persian Gulf War, however, that they were finally tested in combat.

The performance of the land attack cruise missiles was of interest to more than just the United States. Since the late 1970s, the U.S. cruise missile program has attracted the attention of defense officials around the world. Because cruise missiles can strike targets at long ranges, it was recognized that they could supplement or replace manned aircraft for many strategic missions.

Until the late 1980s, much of the technology needed to produce accurate land attack cruise missiles was available to only a few countries other than the United States, such as France and the Soviet Union. Today, however, the technologies to develop these missiles are so widespread that even Third World countries can contemplate their production.

The prospect that the Third World might seek to acquire land attack cruise missiles has been a growing concern.[2] It is clear that Third World countries are becoming increasingly interested in long-range missiles. During the 1980s, the proliferation of ballistic missiles in the Third World reached epidemic proportions. Third World countries purchased ballistic missiles in large quantities, and many committed substantial resources to indigenous ballistic missile development programs. By 1990, more than a dozen nations in the Third World were trying to build their own ballistic missiles.

In this respect, the proliferation of antiship cruise missiles (ASCMs) is significant, for ASCMs can be transformed into land attack weapons with relatively little difficulty. The U.S. Navy has developed two ASCMs, the Harpoon and the Tomahawk, and both exist in land attack versions. ASCMs, which are launched from coast defense batteries, aircraft, surface ships, and submarines, have proliferated even more than ballistic missiles. Although one ASCM can cost $800,000 or more, 40 Third World countries now operate them. Even nations with highly sophisticated strike aircraft want antiship cruise missiles.

Part of the explanation for their spread is the willingness of the countries producing ASCMs to export them with few, if any, restrictions. It is noteworthy that only a handful of Third World countries build antiship cruise missiles, despite the widespread demand. Because ASCMs are so easily acquired, most Third World nations find no reason to manufacture their own. Although at least five countries in the Third World are known to have indigenous programs, many more rely on ASCMs acquired from other Third World countries.

Until recently, few Third World countries had the technology to produce any kind of cruise missile. The obstacles to the development of land attack cruise missiles were especially substantial, and better alternatives appeared to exist. Ballistic missiles and manned strike aircraft were preferred by Third World countries with the opportunity to acquire them. This has started to change. The growing availability of high-accuracy guidance technology, especially satellite navigation systems, should enable Third World countries to produce cruise missiles with accuracies of 100 meters and probably much less. At the same time, Third World countries are gaining access to the airframe and warhead technology needed to make small cruise missiles. It now seems inevitable that Third World countries will begin to acquire land attack cruise missiles during the 1990s.

The spread of antiship cruise missiles indicates, however, that there is no desire to prevent the spread of all types of cruise missiles. ASCMs are exported by almost every major arms supplier, including the United States, France, Great Britain, and Italy. Although the United States works to prevent the proliferation of certain kinds of cruise missile systems, it encourages its allies and friends in the Third World to acquire other types. This ambiguity is at the heart of the dilemma facing efforts to prevent the proliferation of potentially destabilizing cruise missiles.

The Problem of Missile Proliferation

By the early 1990s, it was widely recognized that the spread of long-range surface-to-surface missiles in the Third World had become a serious problem.[3] During the 1980s, many Third World countries had assigned a high priority to the acquisition of ballistic missiles. By 1991, more than 20 of these nations either possessed ballistic missiles or were attempting to obtain them. Several factors motivate Third World countries to seek such weapons. Some countries want them for prestige, others because of their perceived deterrence value. Still others, however, have found that ballistic missiles are capable of assuming critical operational military roles for which no substitutes are available, especially for countries unable to rely on an air force to undertake deep-strike missions.[4]

The proliferation of ballistic missiles has been accelerated by the emergence of production capabilities in the Third World. Although many countries continue to rely on imported missiles, the U.S. intelligence community has estimated that as many as 15 Third World countries could be producing ballistic missiles by the year 2000. Many of these countries are interested in weapons with considerable range. According to Judge William Webster, former director of the Central Intelligence Agency (CIA), "by the year 2000, at least six countries will have missiles with ranges of up to 3,000 kilometers." Moreover, he noted, "at least three of them may develop missiles with ranges of up to 5,500 kilometers."[5]

It is believed that the countries attempting to develop medium- (1,000 to 2,500 kilometers) and intermediate-range (2,500 to 5,500 kilometers) missiles include Brazil, India, Iraq, Israel, Saudi Arabia, and South Africa.[6] No Third World country currently has a missile with a range of more than 3,000 kilometers. India is the only Third World nation known to be interested in developing a ballistic missile with a longer range. It is unclear which other countries might want missiles with such long ranges, but possible candidates include Iraq, Israel, and South Africa.

These weapons were acquired to be used. At least six Third World countries have launched ballistic missiles at adversaries. Seven countries have been the target of these ballistic missiles.[7]

Concern for missile proliferation extends to other systems as well. Not only can ballistic missiles take various forms, some with radically different operational character-istics, but also other, completely different types of long-range surface-to-surface weaponry exist. Indeed, there are five distinct types of long-range land attack weapons: long-range rocket artillery, ballistic missiles, ballistic missiles with guided reentry vehicles, semiballistic missiles, and cruise missiles. In the Third World, there are development programs for weapons in each of these categories. From this perspective, cruise missile proliferation is only one part of a larger trend. Although cruise missiles have unique characteristics, Third World countries have adopted many approaches to the acquisition of long-range land attack munitions.

Rocket Artillery

Unguided ground-launched rockets with ranges of up to 100 kilometers are most commonly used to support frontline combat units. First popularized as the Katyusha by the Soviet Union during World War II, artillery rockets are relatively inexpensive and easy to operate, making it possible to fire them in large numbers in short periods of time. Examples of rocket artillery include the Brazilian ASTROS II SS-60 rockets (60-kilometer range) and the U.S. MLRS (30-kilometer range). The growing sophistication of Third World defense industries has resulted in a large number of rocket artillery development programs for systems with ranges of more than 40 kilometers.

Ballistic Missiles

These unmanned rockets are powered during the initial boost stage, but not during the descent. Once gravity takes over, they follow a curved (or ballistic) trajectory. Long-range ballistic missiles fly outside the atmosphere. Although they are normally fired from ground or submarine launchers, it is possible to build air-launched systems. By 1991, more than a dozen Third World countries were known to be developing ballistic missiles – among them, Argentina, Brazil, Egypt, India, Iran, Iraq, Israel, Libya, North Korea, Pakistan, South Africa, South Korea, and Taiwan.

Ballistic Missiles with Terminally Guided Reentry Vehicles

The accuracy of ballistic missiles can be significantly enhanced by equipping them with guided reentry vehicles. Various guidance techniques can be used, but it is extremely difficult to master the technologies needed to produce them. A radar terrain comparison system developed by the United States for the Pershing II missile made possible a circular error probable (CEP) of less than 50 meters, meaning that half the missiles would land within 50 meters of the target. Indian officials have expressed an interest in developing such systems, and other countries may be pursuing related or different technologies.

Semiballistic Missiles

A variant of the ballistic missile, semiballistic missiles alter direction and velocity after launch. Such systems typically use the fuselage of the missile as a maneuvering body and can be built to ranges of at least 700 kilometers. Examples include the U.S. ATACMS (estimated range, 150 kilometers) and possibly the Soviet SS-21 (estimated range, 70 kilometers). The canceled 500-kilometer Follow-on-to-the-Lance (FOTL) would have been a semiballistic missile. It is possible that the Indian Prithvi, which has a range of about 250 kilometers, is a semiballistic system.

Cruise Missiles

Cruise missiles operate like aircraft, relying on aerodynamic (rather than ballistic) flight and often (but not always) using air-breathing propulsion. Essentially, they are unmanned kamikazes. The first effective cruise missile was the German V-1 used during World War II. ASCMs started to become common during the 1960s. More recently, the United States and the former Soviet Union deployed a large number of strategic and tactical cruise missiles for land attack, many armed with nuclear weapons. Existing cruise missiles can be fired from submarines, surface ships, aircraft, or ground launchers. As a result of its performance in the 1991 Persian Gulf War, the world's best-known cruise missile is almost certainly the U.S. Navy's Tomahawk system.[8]

Defining Cruise Missiles

There is no single definition for cruise missile. According to one widely accepted definition, "a cruise missile is an unmanned, expendable, armed, aerodynamic, air-breathing, autonomous vehicle."[9] This definition, however, excludes many systems commonly regarded as cruise missiles.

Rocket-powered antiship missiles, for example, are usually regarded as cruise missiles because they operate just like ASCMs with air-breathing engines.[10] The similarities between the turbojet-powered Harpoon and the rocket-powered Exocet missiles are far greater than the differences.[11] Most cruise missiles rely on turbine engines and can attain high subsonic speeds. Some, however, are propeller-driven and fly as slowly as 100 kilometers per hour, whereas others relying on ramjet engines are capable of flying at speeds greater than Mach 3.

Defining cruise missiles too strictly can be problematic in other important respects. It might exclude missiles that have a man in the loop during the terminal attack phase but that otherwise conform to the standard definition. The Harpoon antiship missile is without question a cruise missile, but, strictly defined, the SLAM land attack version of the Harpoon is not. The SLAM has a television terminal guidance system that is operated over a data link by a human operator and so is not autonomous.

Issues of this type apparently led the Soviet Union and

the United States to adopt a looser definition when negotiating the Intermediate-Range Nuclear Forces (INF) Treaty. According to that treaty, a cruise missile is an "unmanned, self-propelled vehicle that sustains flight through the use of aerodynamic lift over most of its flight." Separately, it adds the notion that a cruise missile is a "weapon-delivery vehicle." In other words, the critical distinction is neither the engine nor the guidance. Rather, it is the means of flying that distinguishes a cruise missile from other types of surface-to-surface weaponry. A cruise missile relies on aerodynamic lift to keep it in the air, is powered during most or all of its flight, and has flight controls that allow it to maneuver. In contrast, a ballistic missile is powered only during launch, is generally flown to a high altitude from where it descends by gravity (a "ballistic" trajectory), and usually cannot be guided after the first few moments of flight.

This study uses the definition adopted in the INF Treaty, because the important contrast is between weapons that rely on aerodynamic flight and those that depend on ballistic trajectories. This covers both rocket and air-breathing weapons, as well as systems with either fully autonomous or man in the loop guidance.

No effort is made to categorize the weapons by range. Cruise missiles can be built with ranges as short as 20 kilometers and as long as 3,000 kilometers. Long-range missiles are obviously of more concern than short-range ones, but it is unclear at what range and under what circumstances land attack missiles start to become a problem. One approach was provided by the INF Treaty, which covers missiles with a range of 500 kilometers or more, irrespective of the size or character of the payload. Although this may have been appropriate in the context of East-West concerns in Europe, it has considerably less value in other parts of the world.

Similarly, the Missile Technology Control Regime (MTCR), a multinational agreement to prevent missile proliferation, is concerned only with missiles capable of a range of 300 kilometers or more while carrying at least a 500-kilogram warhead. Even this shorter range may fail to address the problem of long-range land attack weapons from the perspective of many Third World countries. Weapons with ranges of 40 kilometers or less can be strategic in many parts of the Third World, given the small size of many countries and the proximity of major population centers to hostile borders. As a result, most Third World countries do not need weapons with ranges of more than 300 kilometers to strike most potential targets.

The main focus of this study is on weapons with a range of at least 100 kilometers, but no attempt is made to define what constitutes a long-range weapon and so systems with shorter ranges are not overlooked.

Cruise Missile Proliferation

The dangers of ballistic missile proliferation have been analyzed extensively. It is now widely recognized that efforts must be made to control the spread of ballistic missiles. In 1987, the United States and six other countries signed the MTCR to prevent further missile proliferation. The agreement concerns missiles that are capable of attaining ranges of more than 300 kilometers carrying a 500-kilogram warhead. Although often identified with attempts to prevent the proliferation of ballistic missiles, the MTCR explicitly identifies cruise missiles and related technologies as a target of the regime. (The MTCR is discussed in more detail in chapter 6.)[12]

Unfortunately, the potential dangers of cruise missiles in the Third World have been too long ignored. Clearly ballistic missile proliferation was well advanced by the late 1980s, and the trend was recognized around the world. In contrast, the spread of cruise missiles has received less attention, even when they pose a tangible threat. For example, United Nations Security Council Resolution 687, which requires Iraq to eliminate its unconventional weapons programs, contains provisions calling for the destruction of all Iraqi ballistic missiles with a range of 150 kilometers or more.[13] There is no mention of cruise missiles. Yet Iraq claimed to be producing ASCMs with ranges of 200 kilometers and was known to be working on more advanced systems. By banning ballistic missiles but allowing cruise missiles, the Security Council essentially told the Iraqis to focus future weapons development programs on cruise missiles.

WILL THIRD WORLD COUNTRIES SEEK cruise missiles in the 1990s as they did ballistic missiles in the 1980s? The following chapters address this central question. To provide an overview of the existing technology, chapter 2 describes the characteristics and capabilities of modern cruise missiles developed in the United States and elsewhere. Chapter 3 then assesses the extent to which Third World countries will be capable of producing comparable systems. Chapter 4 considers the impact of the current revolution in missile guidance technology on proliferation, and chapter 5 examines the Third World's access to the technologies needed to design and manufacture cruise missiles. Finally, chapter 6 focuses on the various responses of the United States and other countries to cruise missile proliferation, including agreements on export controls and arms control.

To provide a baseline for evaluating global trends in development, appendix A summarizes the better-known cruise missile systems in the United States, Great Britain, France, and Germany. The tables of appendix B identify missile systems and critical components that have been produced in the Third World and elsewhere, by country.

It is recognized that the Third World is not homogeneous and that technological capabilities vary considerably from one country to another. Moreover, within a country the level of sophistication can vary from one technology to another. Thus, a nation with overall superior technology may be unable to produce certain items or may have less capability than other Third World countries with generally inferior technological skills.

An effort is made to provide some insight into three key questions. First, to what extent do Third World countries currently use cruise missiles? Second, to what extent are Third World countries currently capable of designing and manufacturing cruise missiles? And third, are there operational roles that might make cruise missiles a particularly attractive option for Third World military forces? There are no definitive answers to these questions. Third World countries rarely provide information about their weapons development programs. Indeed, the first indication that a country is working on a particular system may be the actual appearance of the weapon. Even when data are available, they are often scanty, scattered, and sometimes incorrect. As a result, there are real limitations on any assessment that must rely on open sources of information.

Matters are further complicated by the necessarily speculative nature of this study. Although it is possible to identify Third World countries that appear to be working on cruise missile systems, this is insufficient. At least a few countries with no current interest in cruise missiles are almost certain to initiate development programs during the 1990s. Moreover, countries that seem to lack the requisite technology may be able to initiate development programs by relying on foreign technical assistance. For these reasons, the analysis that follows is intended mainly to illuminate the emerging trends.

2

The Cruise Missile

Cruise missiles are becoming increasingly prominent in the arsenals of modern military forces. During the 1970s, the United States pioneered in the development of a new generation of highly accurate cruise missiles capable of attacking a variety of targets. The potential effectiveness of these missiles was demonstrated for the first time during the 1991 Persian Gulf War. At present, the United States has six known cruise missile programs, although additional classified projects may exist. Moreover, other countries, including some in the Third World, may also have cruise missile programs. As a result, the importance of these weapons is expected to grow as additional systems with greater capability enter service.

Types of Cruise Missiles

Cruise missiles can appear in several different guises. There is a tendency to view cruise missiles only as strategic weapons armed with nuclear warheads, but in reality there are at least four types: (1) strategic cruise missiles, like the U.S. ALCM and Tomahawk TLAM-N missiles, armed with nuclear weapons; (2) antiship cruise missiles, similar to the

U.S. Harpoon, the French Exocet, or the Soviet Styx; (3) conventionally armed ground attack missiles for use against ground targets, such as the U.S. Tomahawk TLAM-C and SLAM systems used against Iraq; and (4) harassment drones, equipped with specialized sensors to detect and attack electronic emitters or armored vehicles, like the Israeli Harpy or the German KDH. Also discussed are remotely piloted vehicles (RPVs), although they are not cruise missiles. Normally used for reconnaissance, RPVs are not attack weapons. They also differ from cruise missiles in other important respects. Remotely piloted vehicles usually are not expendable and are rarely armed. Understanding them, however, is essential in a study of cruise missiles. Many of the technologies needed to develop an RPV are similar to those required for a cruise missile. Indeed, some RPVs are designed so that they can be given warheads and thus can be converted into cruise missiles.

Strategic Cruise Missiles

The United States, France, and the former Soviet Union now operate nuclear-armed cruise missiles for their strategic forces. Although the United States deployed some nuclear-armed cruise missiles in the 1950s and the 1960s, it was only in the 1980s that these weapons became a significant component of the U.S. strategic arsenal. The United States currently has the AGM-86B air-launched cruise missile (ALCM) and the BGM-109 Tomahawk family of ship-launched (SLCM) and ground-launched cruise missile (GLCM). In addition, a new, more stealthy strategic cruise missile, the AGM-129 Advanced Cruise Missile (ACM), will enter service in the next few years.

France now relies on ASMP air-launched cruise missiles to extend the capabilities of the aircraft component of its Force de Frappe. It also has started development of a successor weapon, the ASLP. Great Britain has expressed an interest in acquiring either the ASLP or a similar type of system for its strategic nuclear forces.

The former Soviet Union has operated a large number of nuclear-armed cruise missiles since at least the early 1960s. This includes versions of the SS-N-3 Shaddock, SS-N-12 Sandbox, and SS-N-19 Shipwreck naval missiles, as well as the AS-2 Kipper, AS-3 Kangaroo, AS-4 Kitchen, and AS-6 Kingfish air-launched missiles. There is a new family of strategic cruise missiles, apparently based on a single design, including the air-launched AS-15 Kent and the submarine-launched SS-N-21 Sampson. The Soviets were forced to abandon a ground-launched version, the SSC-X-4, because it was banned under the INF Treaty. These missiles are similar to the nuclear-armed versions of the U.S. Tomahawk.

The former Soviet Union also was developing a second family of considerably larger cruise missiles. The air-launched AS-X-19 and the submarine-launched SS-NX-24 were expected to enter service in the 1990s.[1] The AS-X-19/SS-NX-24 missiles may be the BL-10, which is the designation of a ramjet-powered strategic cruise missile reportedly capable of flying at greater than Mach 2 with a range of 3,200 kilometers.[2]

Antiship Cruise Missiles

ASCMs are manufactured in at least 13 countries, including several in the Third World. More than 70 countries possess ASCMs.[3] Among the systems now in service are the British Sea Eagle, the French Exocet, the Israeli Gabriel (and its South African and Taiwanese derivatives), the Italian OTOMAT, the Swedish RBS-15, and the U.S. Harpoon and Tomahawk. Both the Chinese and the Soviets developed a large number of different systems, many of which have been exported to Third World countries.

The special characteristics of the cruise missile have adapted themselves well to the antiship mission. Antiship missiles rely on terminal guidance systems that have been specifically designed for use against ships. Such systems are intended to give antiship missiles perfect accuracy, allowing them to hit small targets at relatively long ranges because near-misses against ships do little damage. The terminal guidance systems used on antiship missiles include active and semiactive radar, radar-homing, infrared, television, and home-on-jam. ASCMs can rely on either air-breathing engines, such as the turbojets used in the Harpoons, or rocket motors, as used with the Exocets.

ASCMs are now the most important naval weapons in the inventories of most countries. Even relatively small ships can carry a large number of the missiles, each of which is capable of inflicting extensive damage to much larger naval combatants. For example, Israel's 450-ton Reshef-class missile boats typically are armed with four Harpoon and six Gabriel antiship missiles. Any of these missiles can incapacitate a frigate or destroyer weighing 5,000 tons, although sinking the ships may require multiple hits. The punch provided by ASCMs has made it possible for Third World countries to maintain relatively powerful naval forces that rely on comparatively inexpensive missile-armed patrol boats or small corvettes.

Tactical Land Attack Cruise Missiles

During the late 1980s, the United States and France developed new tactical land attack cruise missiles, which were to be procured in large quantities. These missiles can be used when strike aircraft are not available, or they can be fired at high-value targets too heavily defended for manned aircraft to attack successfully. Alternatively, land attack cruise missiles can support air attacks by hitting enemy air defenses.

The performance of the Tomahawk TLAM missiles during the 1991 Persian Gulf War appears to have enhanced the attractiveness of land attack cruise missiles, especially to countries that previously had demonstrated little interest in them. The growing availability of small, inexpensive turbojet engines has made it relatively easy to develop missiles that are capable of long ranges. At present, only a few tactical cruise missiles are in service or under development, but the number will grow during the 1990s.

The U.S. military now operates the TLAM and SLAM land attack cruise missiles but intends to rely more heavily on such weapons in the 1990s. Currently under development is the Tri-Service Standoff Attack Munition (TSSAM), a secret $15 billion program revealed in mid-1991. This weapon will have a range of between 185 and 600 kilometers and will be fired from navy and air force aircraft and army MLRS launchers.[4] There may be additional programs that still remain secret.

The only other Western country with a land attack cruise missile program is France, which expects to field its air-launched Apache in 1996. The Apache has a range of 150 kilometers, but an 800-kilometer-range version of the system also is under development.[5] Sweden is known to be considering production of a land attack cruise missile.[6] Germany and Italy have explored the acquisition or development of such systems.

Harassment Drones

Harassment drones are missiles that loiter over the battlefield while waiting for a target to appear. After detecting a target, the missile halts its search and crashes into the target. The long endurance of cruise missiles makes them well suited for this kind of mission. Two types of harassment cruise missiles have been developed: antiradiation cruise missiles (ARMs) to attack systems that emit electronic signals, such as radar and communications antennae, and specialized land attack cruise missiles to attack armor or self-propelled artillery.

A considerable number of antiradiation harassment drones are now under development, but few are in service. Although the United States has developed several systems, it is not known to have procured any of them in large quantities. Among the systems built during the 1980s was the

Tacit Rainbow, a jet-propelled weapon that can be launched from either aircraft or MLRS launchers. The United States is known to have canceled two propeller-driven antiradiation missile systems, the Pave Tiger and the Seek Spinner. Germany is known to be developing the KDAR, but it is not expected to enter service for several more years. Israel reportedly has deployed at least one antiradiation harassment drone, the Harpy.

Antiradiation harassment drones are a complement to rocket-powered antiradiation missiles, not a replacement. The cruise missiles are slower, sometimes considerably so. The U.S. Harm antiradiation missile is a supersonic weapon, whereas the Israeli Harpy flies at speeds of less than 200 kilometers per hour. The slow speed and long endurance of harassment drones enable them to loiter for extended periods of time to deter enemy use of emitters.[7]

The only antitank harassment drone known to be under serious consideration is the German KDH (Kampfdrohne des Heeres), intended to attack tanks and self-propelled artillery.[8] The KDH, which is capable of attacking only one tank, will probably not be widely accepted. Because tanks rarely move individually, it makes more sense to rely on weapons that can attack a large number of armored vehicles at the same time. In contrast to the KDH, the U.S. Army's TSSAM will deliver a number of Brilliant Anti-Tank (BAT) submunitions to the target area (the exact number is classified).[9] Each TSSAM should be able to destroy several tanks simultaneously.

The Advantages of Cruise Missiles

Although they cannot replace aircraft or ballistic missiles, cruise missiles have unique characteristics giving them distinct advantages over competing types of weapons.[10] The small size of cruise missiles makes it possible for them to be launched from small ships or trucks. This is especially important for naval missions, because it means that all combatants now have standoff strike capabilities, not just aircraft carriers.

Cruise missiles also are capable of achieving high accuracies even at long ranges. They can evade air defenses, exploiting the small size of modern cruise missiles and their ability to fly at extremely low altitudes. Moreover, cruise missiles can maneuver, making it possible for them to fly around enemy air defenses and thus increase their survivability. Many of these advantages derive from the use of small, fuel-efficient turbojet engines.

Accuracy

Modern guidance systems have made it possible to design highly accurate cruise missiles. According to one estimate, the Tomahawk TLAM has a circular error probable or CEP of no more than six meters, although others claim that it can achieve even higher accuracies.[11] New cruise missiles now under development will be capable of accuracies of one meter. (Guidance issues are discussed in more detail in chapter 4.) The strategic significance of accuracy was demonstrated by the destruction wrought on Iraq by U.S. precision-guided munitions. The delivery of highly accurate weapons makes it possible to inflict severe damage on a target set with only conventional munitions.

The available evidence suggests that highly accurate, long-range cruise missiles can be developed more easily than accurate ballistic missiles. Although the United States and the former Soviet Union have developed accurate intercontinental ballistic missiles at a high cost, no Third World country is capable of producing comparable systems. A typical Third World ballistic missile is the Scud-B, which has a CEP of about 1,000 meters at a range of 300 kilometers. A more capable system, the Indian Prithvi, has a range of 250 kilometers and a CEP of only 250 meters.[12] Although it may be possible for Third World countries to produce more accurate ballistic missiles, there is reason to believe that it will be extremely hard for them to make significant improvements.

In contrast, it appears to be much easier technically to produce cruise missiles capable of meter accuracies. With reliance on aerodynamic flight, the path of a cruise missile can be adjusted continuously. In contrast, ballistic missiles are guided only during the first few moments of flight. If the guidance system permits even small deviations from the intended flight path, a ballistic missile might miss its target by a large distance. To prevent such problems, it is necessary to rely on highly precise guidance systems of types not available to any Third World country. Highly accurate ballistic missiles thus are precision instruments of considerable sophistication and cost.[13]

On the other hand, several Third World countries appear to have developed short-range cruise missiles capable of high accuracies. Given current developments in satellite navigation technology, it is likely that Third World countries will be able to construct navigation systems capable of accuracies of at least 100 meters. They may even build cruise missiles with accuracies of less than 10 meters.

Evading Air Defenses

To be effective, a cruise missile must survive hostile air defenses. During World War II, the Allies were able to deploy highly effective defenses against German V-1 cruise missiles. Typically, the V-1s flew at an altitude of between 650 and 750 meters. Although this was lower than anticipated by the British, the missiles were sufficiently high to be detected and engaged with considerable success. For example, the Germans fired 2,759 V-1s at the Belgian port of Antwerp, but 1,766 were destroyed.[14] Similarly, during the 1973 Arab-Israeli War, Egypt reportedly launched 25 AS-5 Kelt air-to-surface missiles at Israeli targets. All but five were shot down by Israeli fighters or antiaircraft weapons. These missiles were launched at an altitude of 9,000 meters, generally from inside Egyptian territory. The AS-5 can fly at relatively low altitudes, but this nearly halves the range of the missile.[15] In both cases, air defenses were able to spot most of the missiles and destroy them.

This experience emphasizes the importance of cruise missile designs that minimize the effectiveness of air defenses. Designers have adopted four techniques to reduce vulnerability. First, modern U.S. cruise missiles now fly at extremely low altitudes, generally under 30 meters. Second, and alternatively, some cruise missiles fly supersonically at high altitudes, out of the reach of most air defense weapons. Third, to further complicate efforts to detect and track cruise missiles, stealth technology is used. Finally, many cruise missiles can be programmed to fly around air defense sites.

Most modern cruise missiles fly at low altitudes. For example, many ASCMs are sea-skimming weapons capable of flying as low as 1.5 meters above the water, although altitudes of 20 meters are more typical. Similarly, the strategic cruise missiles developed by the United States are designed to fly over land at extremely low altitudes. The Tomahawk TLAM reportedly can cruise at less than 30 meters.[16] According to one source, the altitude of the ALCM depends on the terrain. Over water or flat land, the missile can fly as low as 20 meters. Over moderately rough terrain, however, the altitude is increased to 50 meters and over mountains, to 100 meters.[17]

Low-altitude flights complicate the task of the defense. The range at which a ground-based radar can spot a missile is reduced significantly against low-altitude targets. The curvature of the earth automatically limits range, and obstacles such as hills, mountains, and even buildings can block coverage at low altitudes as well. In addition, a missile flying at low altitudes can be masked from radar detection by ground clutter—that is, radar signals reflected from the ground itself.

Even if it is possible to detect a low-flying missile, it may not be possible to destroy it. Few medium- and long-range SAMs are capable of engaging targets flying lower than 50 meters. For example, because the minimum-engagement altitude for the Soviet SA-6 is only 50 meters, it might not be able to engage TLAM or ALCM cruise missiles.[18] Even when a SAM can operate at low altitudes, terrain masking may prevent it from detecting or tracking a target. In other words, the line of sight to a low-altitude target can be blocked by low hills, buildings, or other obstacles. Few SAMs appear equipped to engage low-flying cruise missiles. If this is so, then air defenses are left to defend specific locations against cruise missile attacks with antiaircraft artillery and short-range SAMs. The only currently deployed SAM believed capable of engaging low-flying cruise missiles at medium ranges is the Soviet SA-10.

Cruise missiles also can employ technologies that make it harder for air defenses to detect a missile. Stealth techniques are technically called low observables, because they reduce the chances of detection but do not make a system invisible. The United States incorporated low-observable technology into the ALCM and Tomahawk cruise missiles developed during the 1970s. Although estimates vary, the radar cross section of the ALCM is probably no more than 0.05 square meters. The AGM-129A Advanced Cruise Missile, a stealthy follow-on to the ALCM, will have an even smaller radar cross section. By comparison, the F-4 fighter has a radar cross section of about 6 square meters and the B-1B bomber has one of approximately 0.75 square meters.[19]

Adoption of stealth technology makes it considerably harder to detect a weapon. As demonstrated by the performance of the F-117A stealth fighter during the 1991 Persian Gulf War, a stealthy aircraft is hard to find even at medium altitudes. Integrating low-observable technologies into a missile capable of flying at low altitudes may result in a weapon that is impossible to detect with existing air defense radars.

The significance of low-observable technologies, however, goes beyond the difficulty of detecting a weapon. Even if a stealthy weapon is discovered, it may be impossible for air defense systems to shoot it down. The effectiveness of modern air defense systems depends on the quality of fire control systems that direct surface-to-air missiles and antiaircraft guns. One Soviet analyst expressed considerable skepticism about the ability of most SAMs to engage cruise missiles. According to this assessment, cruise missiles with radar cross sections as low as 0.1 square meters are difficult for SAM fire control radars to track. As a result, even if a SAM battery knows that a cruise missile is present, it may not be able to get a strong enough lock on the target to shoot it down. Even infrared tracking devices may not detect a cruise missile, and SAMs that use infrared guidance may not home onto the cruise missile.[20]

Alternatively, it is possible to design cruise missiles that fly supersonically at high altitudes. The former Soviet Union built several weapons of this type. For example, the AS-6 Kingfish attains speeds as high as Mach 3.5 at a cruising altitude of 18,000 meters. It has a maximum range of nearly 650 kilometers.[21] Similarly, the French ASMP – another Mach 3.5 missile – has a range of 250 kilometers at high altitudes and executes a terminal dive when it reaches the target. The ASMP is also capable of a Mach 2 low-altitude approach, but this reduces the maximum range to only 80 kilometers.[22]

High-altitude supersonic missiles stress air defenses, which are optimized against targets flying at subsonic or low supersonic speeds while at low to medium altitudes. The effectiveness of supersonic, high-altitude flight against air defenses is suggested by the success of the U.S. SR-71 reconnaissance aircraft. The SR-71 is a Mach 3.5 aircraft capable of flying at 32,000 meters. Despite numerous overflights of hostile territory, no SR-71 was ever shot down. It must be noted, however, that the SR-71 incorporated stealth technology, which somewhat reduced its radar signature.[23]

Cruise missiles can maneuver; they do not have to approach a target in a straight line. This means that the missiles can be programmed to fly around air defense concentrations. Because most antiaircraft weapons are a threat to cruise missiles only at short ranges, the maneuverability of cruise missiles can reduce significantly the effectiveness of enemy air defenses. A cruise missile also can follow a flight path that makes optimum use of terrain obstructions that might mask the missile from hostile radar.

Engines

Although cruise missiles rely on many types of engines, the use of air-breathing engines permits the production of missiles with long endurance, providing long ranges.[24] An air-breathing engine does not have to carry its own oxygen supply, whereas rocket engines must haul both fuel and a source of oxygen. Many liquid-fueled rockets have separate tanks for fuel and an oxidizer, and solid-fuel rocket motors contain an oxidizer and fuel that have been carefully mixed together. In contrast, the oxygen used by a jet engine is drawn from the air. For this reason, a cruise missile powered by a turbojet engine can generate more energy from the same weight of propellant than can a rocket-powered missile. According to one estimate, the weight of fuel carried by a turbojet-powered cruise missile is only a third that needed by an otherwise identical rocket-propelled missile. The benefits of turbojet-powered cruise missiles over rocket-powered missiles are most evident in systems with ranges of 100 kilometers or more. Such missiles can carry larger warheads over longer ranges, usually at a lower cost.

It is possible to extend the range of rocket-powered cruise missiles simply by converting to turbojet propulsion. The Chinese turbojet-powered C 802 is based on the earlier rocket-powered C 801 missile. The only external difference between the two missiles is the addition of an air intake scoop for the Wopen turbojet engine on the C 802. The use of a turbojet engine, however, reportedly increases the range of the C 802 by 40 percent over that of the C 801 (from 50 to more than 80 kilometers). Similarly, China developed the HY-4 ASCM by taking an HY-2 Silkworm missile and replacing its liquid-fuel rocket motor with a turbojet engine. This increased the missile's effective range from 95 to 135 kilometers.[25]

It appears to be relatively easy to extend the range of a cruise missile by trading off payload for fuel capacity. Matra, a French missile manufacturer, believes that it can extend the range of the Apache air-launched cruise missile from 150 to 800 kilometers simply by reducing the warhead weight from 780 to 400 kilograms and increasing the amount of fuel carried. No other changes in the missile are needed.[26] Similarly, the U.S. Navy was able to increase the range of the U.S. Tomahawk missile from 1,300 to 1,650 kilometers by reducing the weight of the warhead from 450 to 320 kilograms and by improving the engine.[27]

Cruise missiles with air-breathing engines are powered during their entire flight, providing the energy needed for maneuvers while the missile is attacking its targets. In contrast, rocket motors generally burn out after a relatively short time. Most rocket-powered missiles rely on the energy generated during the first few seconds of powered flight. Cruise missiles can be designed to undertake a complex search for a target or can engage a target more than once. They can even strike several different targets. The latest version of the Tomahawk Land Attack Missile, known as the Block III, can attack three targets with submunitions and then crash into a fourth. The targets can be widely separated.[28] Cruise missiles also can loiter over a target area and wait for a target to appear.

Cruise missiles are well suited to launch from aircraft, giving them an important advantage over ballistic missiles. Although the United States has investigated the desirability of producing air-launched ballistic missiles, the complexity of such systems makes it doubtful that any Third World country could design one. In contrast, a considerable number of countries may be able to develop air-launched cruise missiles.[29]

Warheads

It should be easier to develop payloads for cruise missiles than for ballistic missiles. Because cruise missiles fly like manned aircraft, their payloads can be based on the bombs and submunitions developed for aircraft delivery. In contrast, ballistic missile warheads must be more rugged to withstand the stresses imposed by launch and reentry, including high acceleration and supersonic speeds – the longer the range of the missile, the greater the problem. An ICBM warhead must operate at velocities that can exceed Mach 20.

Cruise missiles are particularly well suited to the delivery of chemical and biological weapons. Chemical and biological agents are most effective when released into the air at low altitudes and relatively slow speeds. Cruise missiles can fly slowly over a target at a low altitude, making them better able to disseminate chemical and biological agents than ballistic missiles. Cruise missiles can be fitted with aerosol generators for spreading chemical and biological agents, a simple but efficient dissemination technology. In addition, a cruise missile can be programmed to maneuver near the target so that it distributes the agent in the most efficient manner. The United States is known to have looked into using the Snark cruise missile in such roles as early as 1952.[30] During the 1950s and early 1960s, it worked on systems to spread biological and chemical agents from drones or cruise missiles.[31]

In other circumstances, the rocket-powered cruise missile might have an advantage. It is easier to produce a rocket-powered cruise missile capable of flying at supersonic speeds than to make a supersonic air-breathing cruise missile. It is evident that supersonic cruise missiles also might be useful under some circumstances. Until recently, rocket-propelled missiles also cost less than turbojet-powered missiles, but this advantage is expected to be reduced by the development of inexpensive turbojet engines. In addition, the turbojet engines currently available for cruise missiles are not capable of supersonic flight. In contrast, it is comparatively easy to develop rockets that accelerate to speeds in excess of Mach 1, an important advantage when reaction time is important or the target is mobile.

ATBMs and Air Defenses

The relative attractiveness of cruise missiles may be increased by the availability of antitactical ballistic missile systems (ATBM) capable of intercepting short-range ballistic missiles. Until comparatively recently, ballistic missiles had an assured penetration capability, meaning that once a missile was launched, there was nothing a defender could do to stop the attack. In contrast, air defenses can engage manned aircraft and cruise missiles.

Ballistic missiles travel at high velocities, and most surface-to-air missiles (SAMs) cannot intercept and destroy them. This is a major advantage of ballistic missiles over competing types of weapons, including manned aircraft and cruise missiles. It is also a source of weakness. Because ballistic missiles fly at high altitudes, it is possible to detect and track them at long ranges. Indeed, the strategic importance of ballistic missiles led the United States to develop Defense Support Program satellites, which can detect the launch of ballistic missiles. Using radar and infrared tracking systems, it is now possible to obtain early warning of an impending ballistic missile attack. In addition, ATBM systems can intercept short-range ballistic missiles.

At present, the number of potential suppliers of ATBM systems is limited. The former Soviet Union and the United States both possess ATBMs, but only the United States has supplied such weapons to Third World countries. The United States has sold versions of its Patriot SAM system armed with missiles adapted for the ATBM role. Patriots deployed in Israel and Saudi Arabia during the 1991 Persian Gulf War engaged Iraqi Al-Husayn missiles, although the success of the missile has been disputed. Whatever the real performance of the Patriot, it is evident that ATBM systems are becoming a standard component of sophisticated Third World air defenses.

Additional sources of ATBM weaponry might emerge during the 1990s. Some European countries remain interested in developing ATBM systems and would probably make them available to Third World customers. Moreover, several Third World countries appear to be developing their own ATBM systems, including Iraq (before the Persian Gulf War), Israel, and Taiwan. By the end of the decade, virtually any country with the resources to pay for an ATBM system is likely to acquire one.

The presence of ATBM systems may give an edge to cruise missiles. Theoretically, air defense systems are capable of intercepting cruise missiles, but the air defenses available to the Third World are limited to providing point defenses.

Cruise Missiles in the Persian Gulf War

The first combat test for the new generation of cruise missiles developed by the United States during the 1970s was the 1991 Persian Gulf War. The Pentagon officially reported that 288 Tomahawk TLAM missiles were launched during the war, 276 from surface ships and 12 from submarines.[32] In addition, the U.S. Navy employed in combat for the first time its air-launched SLAM standoff land attack missile. One press report claims that the U.S. Air Force may have secretly deployed two additional types of cruise missiles.[33]

A U.S. Department of Defense assessment concluded that the TLAMs were "highly successful," although it observed: "On the basis of a preliminary assessment, strategic targets struck by the Tomahawk suffered at least moderate damage. The level of damage contributed by individual missiles is difficult to discern in instances where multiple missiles were used against the same aimpoint." According to this account, the TLAM was valuable for several reasons. First, it "freed Coalition aircraft for other missions that could be better executed by manned aircraft." Second, Tomahawk could "strike multiple objectives when weather conditions restricted other precision munitions." And finally, it made possible daylight attacks on Baghdad "without endangering pilots or requiring large support efforts."[34] These preliminary conclusions may be modified after more extensive study.

At the start of the Persian Gulf War, the U.S. Navy ships in the Persian Gulf and the Red Sea were armed with 477 TLAM-C and TLAM-D missiles. These weapons were deployed on battleships, cruisers, destroyers, and submarines.[35] Of the 288 missiles fired during the war, only 6 failed during the launch process. Press reports suggest that only 85 percent of the TLAMs fired actually struck their targets.[36] No explanations have been given for the failure of approximately 42 missiles.

TLAM strikes were an integral part of the offensive launched against Iraq during the first hour of the fighting on January 16. During the first 24 hours, 106 TLAMs were deployed. The first wave of 52 missiles was fired from surface ships in the Persian Gulf and was directed against targets that would assist the penetration of the initial air strikes. Pentagon sources claimed that 50 TLAMs struck their targets.[37] To cover the egress of the strike aircraft, a second wave of 54 TLAMs was fired. In all, 100 of the 106 missiles launched during those two waves were considered successful.[38]

It appears that approximately 100 more TLAMs were employed on the second day of the war, but that launch rates dropped dramatically thereafter. According to one U.S. official, "Two-thirds of the Tomahawks were fired in the first two days." The early success of the air campaign made extensive additional use of the TLAMs unnecessary. As a result, mission planners decided to husband the remaining missiles and significantly reduced the rates of fire.[39] The last TLAM was launched on February 2, well before the fighting ended.

Pentagon sources claim that every TLAM target was

struck, owing to the tactics used during the war. Typically, two or three missiles were fired in succession at each target. Although the high success rate made this a wasteful practice, it ensured that no targets escaped unscathed.[40]

A wide range of targets were struck using TLAMs. The Pentagon states that the missiles were fired at "command and control headquarters, power generation facilities, and strategic infrastructure." Press reports suggest that targets included chemical weapons production facilities, ammunition manufacturing facilities, aircraft shelters, and air base runways. According to one report, a TLAM was able to destroy a hardened aircraft shelter by penetrating through a door on the side of the structure.[41] Four missiles hit the headquarters of the Iraqi Ministry of Defense. A concentration of 40 TLAMs was directed at an unidentified ammunition production complex consisting of numerous separate buildings.[42]

Many of the missiles were aimed at targets in the heavily defended Baghdad area. According to some accounts, the air master plan called for night attacks on Baghdad using F-117A stealth fighters to be supplemented by TLAM strikes during the day. This ensured that round-the-clock attacks were mounted on the Iraqi capital.

The U.S. Navy claims that no Tomahawk missiles were shot down by Iraqi air defenses.[43] But Iraqi officials, supported by the observations of some Western journalists stationed in Baghdad during the fighting, claim that Iraqi antiaircraft guns shot down at least a few of the missiles.[44]

The Future of the Cruise Missile

Cruise missiles have come of age. They are adaptable weapons capable of undertaking a variety of critical military missions. It is now possible to build cruise missiles with long ranges and extreme accuracies. The latest version of the conventionally armed Tomahawk TLAM-C missile has a range of up to 1,650 kilometers yet can strike within a few meters of the aimpoint. Experience in the Persian Gulf War has shown that the missiles work.

There is ample evidence that cruise missiles will become even more important in the future. The United States and other countries are developing a new generation of these missiles that will be more accurate than existing systems. Moreover, the new weapons will take advantage of improvements in sensor technology, making it possible for them to attack certain types of mobile targets, such as armored vehicles or trucks.

3

Cruise Missiles in the Third World

Countries in the Third World first acquired cruise missiles during the early 1960s, when the former Soviet Union started exporting SS-C-2 Styx antiship missiles. Since then, antiship cruise missiles have become an integral part of the military forces of Third World countries. These nations have purchased large quantities from foreign suppliers, and several of them have developed the capacity to produce their own.

Despite the widespread acceptance of ASCMs, few cruise missiles capable of performing other roles have appeared in the Third World. Only a handful of countries have acquired or attempted to develop land attack cruise missiles or harassment drones. So far as is known, no strategic cruise missiles exist in the Third World.

It is too early to tell what lessons Third World countries have drawn from the events of the 1991 Persian Gulf War. Even before the war, there were indications of their growing interest in land attack cruise missiles. There was no evidence, however, that the proliferation of land attack cruise missiles was likely to be as extensive as that of ballistic missiles and ASCMs. The Persian Gulf War is certain to affect the attitudes of Third World countries concerning the relative value of ballistic missiles as compared with cruise missiles. Military experts in the Third World were acutely aware of the dramatic contrast between the inaccuracy of the Iraqi Al-Husayn ballistic missiles and the performance of the U.S. Tomahawk cruise missiles.

Nevertheless, it is not yet possible to determine whether Third World countries view events of the Persian Gulf War as a demonstration of the military utility of land attack cruise missiles. This makes it impossible to predict with certainty whether or not Third World countries will embark on programs to acquire or develop these weapons. Past experience suggests, however, that if Third World countries decide that land attack cruise missiles will contribute to their security, they will make every effort to acquire them.

Acquisition of Cruise Missiles

Third World countries can obtain cruise missiles either from foreign suppliers or through indigenous production. A number of countries outside the Third World build cruise missiles and have shown a willingness to export them. Suppliers of cruise missiles to the Third World have included China, France, Great Britain, Italy, the former Soviet Union, and the United States. Almost all the cruise missiles exported have been ASCMs or antiradiation weapons. None of these countries is known to have supplied land attack cruise missiles to the Third World, nor is there reason to believe that they will readily export such weapons in the future. The growing acceptance of the Missile Technology Control Regime, which imposes restrictions on the export of cruise missiles and cruise missile technology, is likely to prevent many cruise missile exports. As a result, it will be difficult for Third World countries to acquire land attack cruise missiles from the traditional suppliers of ASCMs. Many of the weapons, such as the French Apache, could not be exported without violating the 300-kilometer range and 500-kilogram payload ceiling set by the MTCR.[1] Thus, it is unlikely that land attack exports will follow the pattern set by ASCM transfers.

Countries that are not a party to the MTCR may be more willing to sell long-range cruise missiles. China and North Korea, for example, continue to export ballistic missiles despite efforts by the United States and other countries to prevent such shipments. Given that several countries producing ASCMs are not regulated by the MTCR, some countries might be willing to export land attack cruise missiles as well.

It is also possible that cruise missile development programs could follow the same pattern that emerged with ballistic missile proliferation. Although many countries rely on imported ballistic missiles, a significant number have established their own development projects. For a variety of reasons, even countries with access to foreign missiles have been willing to expend the resources needed to design and produce indigenous systems. If Third World countries want land attack cruise missiles and find that they cannot acquire them from existing producers, they will attempt to make the missiles themselves.

Complete weapons can be built relying on components and production expertise provided by a foreign supplier. Such weapons are essentially identical to the ones produced by the original manufacturer. This approach is used to acquire proficiency in production technology, although the local engineering and design input is nonexistent. In other cases, missiles can be built to a foreign specification, but the indigenous producer can rely to some extent on locally produced components. Reliance on indigenous manufacture will depend largely on the capabilities of the local industries and on the relative economic and other advantages of domestic or foreign acquisition of components. In many cases, license-built systems are modified to meet local requirements. Finally, a country may be able to design its own weapons even if it relies heavily on foreign components. The decision depends to some extent on the availability and cost of foreign-supplied subsystems.

No Third World arms industry is totally independent of foreign sources of supply. Indeed, most of these industries are perfectly willing to rely on imported components or even subsystems. Reliance on imports may be reduced because of fears of technology controls or because of a desire to develop an industry of perceived strategic importance. In general, however, Third World countries recognize that economic and technological considerations make the use of imported components and subsystems highly desirable.

The dependence on imports can take many forms. Even countries that invest heavily in research and development recognize that it is impossible to duplicate the output of the industrialized world. Hence, Third World countries try to obtain dual-use civilian technology in addition to the explicitly military technology. Sometimes they obtain the technology legitimately, through direct purchase or through collaborative development programs. All too often, they resort to covert theft of technology.

Antiship Cruise Missiles

ASCMs are now available throughout the Third World. Currently, more than 40 Third World countries possess ASCMs, although only 18 appear to have missiles that rely on air-breathing turbojet engines. Widely exported rocket-powered ASCMs include the French Exocet, the Soviet Styx, and the Chinese Silkworm. Turbojet-powered ASCMs in the inventories of Third World military forces include the U.S. Harpoon, the Italian OTOMAT, and the British Sea Eagle.

Most ASCMs in the inventories of Third World countries were imported from the industrialized countries. Only five countries in the Third World currently manufacture ASCMs or have systems under development. Israel, South Africa, and Taiwan produce cruise missiles relying on both turbojets and solid-fuel rocket motors, and Iraq and North Korea manufacture missiles with liquid-fuel rocket engines. In addition, Brazil and India have programs to develop rocket-powered antiship missiles. Other Third World countries have been willing to rely solely on foreign supplies of antiship missiles.

Israel

The first Third World country to build an antiship missile was Israel. Development of the rocket-powered Gabriel ASCM was dictated by the lack of alternatives. When Israel initiated the Gabriel missile program in the early 1960s, none of its traditional arms suppliers produced a small ASCM.[2] Subsequently, the Israelis exported Gabriel missiles to other Third World countries, including Chile, Ecuador, Kenya, Singapore, and Thailand. South Africa and Taiwan obtained production rights for the Gabriel. Upgraded versions of the missile are now produced in Israel (Gabriel 3), South Africa (Skorpioen), and Taiwan (Hsiung Feng I).[3]

In the late 1970s, Israel considered building another antiship missile to supplement the Gabriel. This was the Flower, a rocket-powered ASCM that Israel intended to develop using Iranian funds.[4] Although some reports have claimed that the Flower was a ballistic missile, in reality it was a supersonic ASCM with a range of 200 kilometers. The country hoped to produce a version that could be launched from submarine torpedo tubes.[5] The fall of the shah, however, eliminated Iran as a potential source of funds and led to cancellation of the program.

Israel Aircraft Industries continued to work on more capable ASCMs. In 1985, details were released for the Gabriel 4, an ASCM with a range of 200 kilometers. The missile has a turbojet engine and can receive target updates from external sources.[6] It is not known whether the Gabriel 4 is operational.

South Africa

South Africa received its first antiship missiles from Israel in the 1970s, along with technology to build the weapons. ARMSCOR, a government-owned company responsible for most weapons production in South Africa, produces the Skorpioen, a license-built version of the Israeli Gabriel 2. However, the South Africans wanted antiship missiles with a longer range than the Skorpioen. In 1986, the chairman of ARMSCOR revealed that his company had "a project to increase the range of sea-to-sea missiles." He also noted that his company had developed "advanced gas-turbine engines" for use in missiles.[7] In 1989, South Africa successfully launched a Skorpioen missile at a target "beyond the horizon."[8] This suggests successful completion of a turbojet-powered antiship missile.

Taiwan

The first ASCM manufactured in Taiwan was a copy of the Israeli Gabriel 2 missile known as the Hsiung Feng I. Like the original, this rocket-powered missile relied on a television guidance system. Subsequently, Taiwan developed an indigenous ASCM known as the Hsiung Feng II. Although Taiwanese officials credit the missile with a range of more than 80 kilometers, at least one source puts the range at 180 kilometers.[9] Recently, Taiwanese officials have claimed that the Hsiung Feng II will "fly farther and faster [than the Harpoon] because it is lighter." This tends to support the reports of a 180-kilometer range, given that the Harpoon has a range of more than 110 kilometers. Ship-launched and coastal defense versions have been developed, and air-launched and submarine-launched versions are under development.[10] The Hsiung Feng II is similar in design to the U.S. Harpoon antiship missile, and it may be based in part on Harpoon technology acquired from the United States in the late 1970s or early 1980s.

Styx Variants

Iraq and North Korea have produced ASCMs derived from the Soviet SS-N-2 Styx, a missile that became operational in the early 1960s. The Styx relies on a liquid-fueled rocket motor. China began to manufacture the Styx as the HY-1 in the mid-1960s and introduced an upgraded version, the HY-2 (better known as the Silkworm, the code name assigned the missile by U.S. intelligence). North Korea has built copies of both the HY-1 and the HY-2. Although it could have obtained similar missiles from either the Soviet Union or China, in the past both countries imposed arms embargoes on North Korea, and the North Koreans prefer to make their own weapons. The missiles probably depend heavily on imported Chinese components, especially the sustainer motors and guidance. North Korea is known to have exported its copies of the HY-2 to Iran and possibly other countries.[11]

Iraq claimed in 1989 that it was producing the Faw family of ASCMs based on the Soviet SS-N-2C Styx antiship missile. The Faw 70, which has a range of 70 kilometers, can accept midcourse guidance correction from external sources. Iraq also claimed that it had two other versions with larger fuel tanks and longer ranges, the Faw 150 with a range of 150 kilometers and the Faw 200 with a range of 200 kilometers.[12]

These variants of the Styx could provide a base for eventual development of land attack cruise missiles. Further, it might be possible to extend the range and endurance of these missiles by adapting them to use turbojet engines in place of the existing rocket motors. China has produced the HY-4, a version of the HY-2 Silkworm with a turbojet engine, increasing the range to 135 kilometers, compared with only 95 kilometers for the HY-2.[13]

Brazil

The Brazilian navy relies totally on foreign-supplied antiship missiles, and it appears to have no requirement for a domestically produced antiship missile. In the mid-1980s, however, a Brazilian arms manufacturer, Avibras, started a development program for an antiship missile. This weapon, probably intended mainly for export, was known as the Barracuda (alternative names were SM-70 and Astros II/

M). It had a range of 70 kilometers and appears to have been based on Avibras Astros II SS-60 artillery rockets. The missile was supposed to be in service in 1989, but Avibras suspended the program—perhaps because of financial problems.[14]

India

India reportedly intends to develop its own short-range ASCM.[15] This missile may be based on the country's Akash surface-to-air missile. Although the Akash is generally described as a medium-range surface-to-air missile, Indian officials have called it a surface-to-surface missile as well.[16] Apparently, the Akash is based on the airframe of India's Soviet-built SA-6 surface-to-air missile. Like the SA-6, the Akash relies on a ramjet motor. Indian sources claim, however, that the engine, like the guidance package, was developed in India. In its surface-to-air role, the missile relies on command guidance.[17] The characteristics of an antiship missile based on the Akash are unclear.

South Korea

The South Korean navy relies exclusively on foreign-built ASCMs. Nevertheless, the country has developed the Sea Dragon, a laser-guided antiship missile with a range of 7 kilometers, with assistance from a U.S. company, Texas Instruments.[18] It is possible that during the 1990s South Korea might decide to construct an indigenous ASCM. At least one South Korean defense expert has supported development of an ASCM with a range of 400 kilometers.[19]

Other Third World Countries

Few Third World countries other than the ones mentioned here are likely to produce ASCMs. The major arms exporting countries have shown themselves quite willing to sell long-range ASCMs. The development of antiship missiles confers little prestige, in contrast to other types of missile systems. Moreover, the quantities required are rarely sufficient to justify indigenous production, and, in most cases, it is less expensive to import the missiles. Accordingly, it is doubtful that many countries will divert resources to develop ASCMs.

Only three circumstances are likely to induce Third World countries to manufacture ASCMs. First, if arms embargoes make it difficult for certain countries to obtain the missiles, such countries may produce them to meet operational requirements. This certainly has been the case for South Africa and Taiwan. It also partially explains North Korea's production of the Silkworm. Second, countries (or companies) that perceive a potential export market, like China and Brazil, are apt to build missiles, even in the absence of domestic demand. Such economic motivations, however, will apply only in a few cases. Third, countries desiring to maintain their independence from foreign sources of supply might be inclined to include antiship missiles in their inventory of indigenously produced weapons. This would be India's reason for building its own missile.

The importance of Third World ASCM programs should not be underestimated. These weapons are readily adaptable to other missions, including land attack. Both ASCMs made by the United States – the naval Tomahawk and the Harpoon – exist in land attack versions. The Harpoon variant, the SLAM, is particularly important in this respect because it illustrates the ease with which the conversion can take place. Relatively few changes in the original design were needed to produce the SLAM. Indeed, Israel's television-guided Gabriel II ASCM and its Taiwanese and South African variants are essentially shorter-range, surface-launched versions of the SLAM. A number of Soviet ASCMs, such as the AS-5 Kelt, also exist in antiradiation versions capable of land attack.[20] The Soviet Union built antiradiation versions of many of its ASCMs. Accordingly, it should be assumed that any country capable of producing an ASCM can produce other short-range cruise missiles as well.

Tactical Land Attack Cruise Missiles

Few programs to develop land attack cruise missiles exist in the Third World, although several Third World countries possess much of the technology needed to manufacture these systems. Others probably could gain access to the necessary technology with little difficulty.

Israel currently manufactures the Popeye, a rocket-powered, television-guided missile. It clearly has the ability to build more capable systems with longer ranges and autonomous guidance systems. Israel's military industries produce airframes, navigation systems, terminal guidance, and engines that are suitable for use in land attack cruise missiles. Some of the technology is rather sophisticated.

Iraq is known to have been working on two land attack cruise missile projects prior to the 1991 Persian Gulf War. The Ababil missile was first shown in 1989, but there is no evidence that it ever entered service with the Iraqi military. Apparently, the Ababil was based on the Italian Mirach series of remotely piloted vehicles. According to one report, the missile was expected to have a range of 500 kilometers while carrying a payload of 250 kilograms. It was fitted with a terminal guidance system employing either an infra-red or a television seeker. The missile was 6 meters long and weighed about 1,000 kilograms.[21]

In addition, Iraq appears to have started development work on a Mach 3 ramjet missile with an estimated range of 650 to 800 kilometers. British sources reported that Iraqi engineers had asked two British companies to run wind tunnel tests on a ramjet in late 1989, when the project was in an early design stage. One expert calculated that it would probably take Iraq a decade to complete development of the system. The British firms apparently refused to run the tests.[22] The current status of the project is unknown, but Iraq's interest in ramjets is significant.

Iranian officials have claimed that they can convert indigenously built mini-RPVs into attack weapons by providing them with warheads.[23] Although it is doubtful that such weapons will be deployed, the statements suggest Iran's awareness of the possibilities of the technology and of the potential virtues of land attack missiles.

Taiwan seems to have the ability to develop such weapons. Because its Hsiung Feng II missile is similar to the Harpoon missile, this country could develop a version of the SLAM. The Hsiung Feng I antiship missile uses a television guidance system, indicating that it may be possible for Taiwan to use TV-terminal guidance. South Africa also has the capability to produce systems like the SLAM. Like the Hsiung Feng I, the Skorpioen antiship missile uses television guidance. This could be coupled with the cruise missile versions of the Skorpioen believed to be under development.[24]

The Indian PTA target drone could be the basis for a land attack cruise missile. It can carry a warhead for use as an attack weapon, and some foreign analysts appear to believe that India intends to incorporate it into a cruise missile.[25] As a target drone, the PTA weighs 650 kilograms, has an engine generating 400 kilograms of thrust, and carries an internal payload of 14 kilograms in addition to the weight of the targets towed by the drone. It has a maximum speed of Mach 0.8 and an endurance of one hour when flying at 7,000 meters at a velocity of 750 kilometers per hour. Indian officials indicated that the PTA was to enter production in 1992, a prediction that appears to have been overly optimistic.[26]

Argentina may be capable of deploying a similar system. Quimar, an Argentine company, is developing the MQ-2 Bigua, a version of the Italian Mirach 100 RPV. The MQ-2 is a multipurpose system that can be used as a target, a decoy, an electronic warfare platform, or a reconnaissance system. In addition, it can be employed as an attack system, although there is no evidence that Argentina has built any weapons for that role.[27]

Despite the evident interest in land attack cruise missiles and the fact that several countries can develop such systems, the only land attack weapon now in service in the Third World appears to be the Israeli Popeye system. There is no evidence that any Third World country has a cruise missile comparable to the U.S. TLAM-C. Whether such weapons emerge in the next few years will depend in large measure on how Third World military forces react to changes in technology that increase the attractiveness of land attack cruise missiles. For example, will these forces exploit the revolution in guidance technology that can provide highly accurate tactical weapons? Or will they largely ignore the potential of precision-guided munitions, as many Third World countries have done since the early 1970s? Equally important, how will such weapons interact with the operational requirements of military forces in the Third World?

Harassment Drones

Harassment drones are highly specialized weapons, and only a few countries have adopted them. Israel is the only Third World country currently known to possess harassment drones. Israel has developed the Harpy antiradiation drone, a propeller-driven system that carries a seeker and a small high-explosive warhead. With a range of more than 500 kilometers, it is designed to detect and home in on radars and communications antennae. The system is sufficiently sophisticated to interest the U.S. Air Force.[28]

In the early 1980s, Israel operated the Delilah, apparently a special-purpose unmanned air vehicle decoy to support electronic warfare operations against early-warning radars and guidance radars for surface-to-air missiles. Produced by Israel Military Industries, the Delilah is a Mach 0.8 missile capable of carrying a payload of 54 kilograms. It can be fired from aircraft or ground launchers. This missile can act as a decoy, simulating the appearance of a manned aircraft. In addition, it can carry electronic deception equipment or chaff to disrupt radar operations. The Delilah was used against Syrian forces during the 1982 Lebanon War.[29]

Harassment drones are difficult to build, as considerable technical expertise is needed to design specialized seekers and to integrate the seekers with the flight controls. Few Third World countries are likely to possess such skills during the next decade.

Strategic Missiles

Several Third World countries already possess strategic weapons, and the number undoubtedly will grow during the coming decade. India, Israel, and Pakistan are generally believed to have nuclear weapons, and several other countries—possibly Iran, Iraq, and North Korea—are thought to be working to develop them. South Africa probably had a nuclear capability prior to signing the nuclear Non-Proliferation Treaty, and several other countries have had weapons development programs, including Brazil.[30]

In addition, Third World countries have programs to acquire chemical and biological weapons. According to one U.S. intelligence estimate, "At least fourteen countries outside of NATO and the Warsaw Pact currently have an offensive chemical weapons capability." This source also claims that "ten more nations are believed to be either developing (or are suspected of seeking) an offensive CW capability." Several of them have produced or are attempting to produce chemical warheads for ballistic missiles, including Iran, Iraq, Israel, Libya, North Korea, and Syria.[31] In all cases, these are considered to be strategic systems.

No Third World country is known to possess missile warheads suitable for delivering biological agents. Dissemination of these agents is difficult, and it may be some time before any Third World nation has a reliable missile delivery system for biological weapons.[32]

It should be noted that conventionally armed cruise missiles can operate as strategic weapons in a Third World context. The "war of the cities" fought between Iran and Iraq, which had a substantial influence on the course of their 1980–1988 conflict, was waged with conventionally armed ballistic missiles. Iran fired Scud-B missiles at Baghdad, as well as short-range Oghab and Nazeat rockets on Iraqi cities near the front lines. Iraq used Al-Husayn missiles, which were extended range versions of the Scud-B, against Tehran and other Iranian cities. It is generally agreed that Iraq's missile attacks played a role in persuading Iran to accept the cease-fire with Iraq in 1988.[33] Iraq also launched conventionally armed Al-Husayn missiles at targets in Israel and Saudi Arabia during the 1991 Persian Gulf War.

Although several Third World countries have an interest in strategic weapons, it is unclear that those countries will rely on cruise missiles for strategic missions. The development of the ALCM and SLCM strategic cruise missiles by the United States in the 1970s resulted from a special confluence of strategic, bureaucratic, and technical considerations. For example, the United States sought cruise missiles to get around some of the restrictions on ballistic missiles imposed by the SALT I Treaty. Thus, it is not self-evident that other countries seeking to acquire strategic missile forces would find cruise missiles equally attractive.

A further impediment to the ready adoption of strategic cruise missiles in the Third World will be the availability of alternative delivery systems. Every Third World country believed to be developing nuclear weapons also has a ballistic missile program.[34] India is developing the Agni 2,500-kilometer missile and is looking into the design of a follow-on with a range of 5,000 kilometers. Israel is known to have the Jericho II, which has a range of at least 1,500 kilometers. South Africa is testing a medium-range missile, probably based on the Jericho – also with a range of 1,500 kilometers. Pakistan is attempting to develop ballistic missiles with ranges of up to 600 kilometers.

Finally, many Third World countries possess long-range strike aircraft. For these countries, the reliability, range, and accuracy of aircraft delivery may outweigh the vulnerability of the strike planes to air defenses. Modern strike aircraft using only unguided "dumb" bombs can deliver ordnance with accuracies of 5 to 15 meters. Precision-guided munitions can reduce this to only 1 meter. Third World air defenses are often too weak to prevent sophisticated strike aircraft from reaching critical targets. Generally, air defenses are capable of shooting down no more than 5 percent of the aircraft engaged.

Nevertheless, cruise missiles might be attractive as strategic weapons in three circumstances. First, they may have an important retaliatory role. Cruise missiles are relatively small and can be launched from a variety of platforms, including submarines, ground-based mobile launchers, and aircraft. As a result, they should be easy to hide and disperse, giving them a second-strike capability.

Second, even countries that intend to rely mainly on manned aircraft to deliver strategic weapons may wish to possess cruise missiles as a means of increasing the effectiveness of strike aircraft. The French, Russians, and Americans depend on cruise missiles to enhance the capabilities of their bombers. In essence, cruise missiles extend the effective range of the launching aircraft by making it possible to strike targets at a distance from the release point. This means that the aircraft fly a shorter distance, using the fuel saved to adopt flight profiles that minimize their vulnerability to hostile air defenses. The aircraft can maneuver around defended localities at lower altitudes, reducing the chances that it will be damaged by enemy air defenses.

Third, cruise missiles give a bomber force enhanced penetration capabilities. The reduced visibility of small cruise missiles may enable them to penetrate heavily defended targets. In addition, cruise missiles can complicate the task of air defenses by increasing the number of potential targets.

These benefits are particularly important for Third World countries. Because they lack the resources to build or acquire a strategic bomber force, they must depend on fighter-bombers acquired from foreign or domestic sources. These aircraft may lack the range needed for many strategic missions.

At least some Third World countries may find cruise missiles to be a useful supplement to existing strategic weapons delivery systems. Some sources have speculated that Israel might be interested in developing a nuclear-armed, submarine-launched cruise missile. Such a weapon could be attractive to a small country like Israel, which lacks space in which to deploy and protect nuclear delivery vehicles. Moreover, Israel might not have sufficient warning time to protect its nuclear delivery capabilities from hostile attack (especially as long-range weapons become more common). In contrast, no Arab country is likely to be able to detect and destroy SLCM-launching submarines until sometime in the twenty-first century.

It is not yet possible to anticipate the potential roles that Third World countries might assign to strategic cruise missiles. Although these missiles have some advantages over alternative delivery systems, they also have disadvantages. In many cases, the potential vulnerability of cruise missiles to air defenses, even if such defenses have a limited capability, may make ballistic missiles more attractive. Moreover, the relatively slow speeds of cruise missiles may not meet operational requirements of strategic forces in the Third World. Finally, many of these nations already have ballistic missile programs and might be unwilling to expend resources on strategic cruise missiles as well.

Conclusion

Cruise missiles have been adopted by the Third World mainly as antiship weapons. Only a few Third World countries are known to have explored land attack cruise missiles or harassment drones. There is no evidence at present that any nation in the Third World has developed a strategic cruise missile. Nevertheless, there is reason to believe that growing numbers of Third World countries will attempt to acquire land attack cruise missiles, including some for strategic missions.

The spread of antiship cruise missiles in the Third World during the 1970s and 1980s provides some important insights regarding the prospects for proliferation of land attack cruise missiles. First, despite the high cost of ASCMs, many Third World countries believed that these weapons had a high military utility. Given their heavy investment in ballistic missiles, it is likely that the potential cost of acquiring land attack cruise missiles will not prevent proliferation. Rather, the perceived utility of these weapons will be critical in any acquisition decision.

Second, if it is not possible to purchase land attack cruise missiles from foreign suppliers, many Third World countries will invest in the resources needed to initiate domestic production. Most of these nations currently import ASCMs, but several have initiated indigenous programs to minimize their dependence on foreign suppliers. Just as Third World countries were willing to invest resources in the development of ballistic missiles, they may be willing to undertake the production of land attack cruise missiles if they cannot acquire them from foreign suppliers.

Third, despite the evident complexity of ASCMs, several Third World countries have produced versions either developed indigenously or based on foreign designs. This suggests that it also may be possible for a number of Third World countries to manufacture land attack cruise missiles.

Ultimately, land attack cruise missiles will proliferate if Third World countries decide that such weapons will enhance their security and if those countries are able to acquire the missiles. At present, the evidence of Third World interest in land attack cruise missiles remains scanty. This makes it almost impossible to predict the potential demand. Nor is it clear that it will be possible for Third World countries to acquire land attack cruise missiles from foreign suppliers. Although a few countries might be willing to export such weapons, many others will not. Consequently, much will depend on the extent to which Third World countries can acquire the requisite technology on their own.

4

Cruise Missile Guidance

The current revolution in missile guidance technology
will contribute significantly to the prospects for cruise missile proliferation. Historically, the most significant obstacles to the design and development of cruise missiles have
been the cost and complexity of guidance systems. Midcourse guidance is needed to get a missile to the immediate
vicinity of the target, and terminal guidance is necessary to
hit the target. Recent advances in technology, especially the
development of satellite navigation systems, are making it
possible for a growing number of countries to produce highly accurate guidance missile systems at extraordinarily low
cost. Thus, the greatest single barrier to the proliferation of
land attack cruise missiles is quickly disappearing.

In the past, the building of small, accurate, and inexpensive guidance systems for cruise missiles was a formida-
ble task. The failure of the first two generations of U.S.
cruise missiles resulted largely from the inadequacies of the
weapons' guidance systems. The technology required to
navigate unmanned platforms with accuracy over long
ranges simply did not exist during the 1940s and 1950s. It
took considerable time, and the development of several generations of new technology, to eliminate most of the obstacles to long-range, autonomous navigation.[1]

Several guidance systems are associated with cruise missiles. Improvements in inertial guidance technology have made available inexpensive and reliable systems suitable for use in cruise missiles. For this reason, all cruise missiles are now equipped with inertial navigation systems (INS) that use gyroscopes to detect changes in relative position. Commercially available INS, suitable for use in light aircraft, are capable of guiding cruise missiles. Specialized INS packages developed for military remotely piloted vehicles also can be used in cruise missiles.

Inertial devices, however, are inherently inaccurate. As a cruise missile flies from one point to another, its INS will report positions that are progressively more distant from the actual location. As a result, a supplemental source of position information is needed to correct for such errors. Several methods have been developed to update midcourse guidance systems, including terrain comparison, satellite, stellar, and radio update systems. Terrain comparison (TERCOM) systems use radar to compare the landscape over which a missile is flying with digital maps stored in a computer. Satellite navigation systems, such as the Global Positioning System (GPS), employ signals transmitted from a constellation of specialized navigation satellites to provide updated position information. Stellar navigation systems automatically track the relative position of easily located stars, essentially performing an automated version of traditional star tracking. Radio update systems come in many forms, but all use land-based transmitters to send signals that can be used to calculate the position of a receiver in relation to the transmitter.

The maturation of digital terrain comparison systems made possible the development of the third generation of U.S. land attack cruise missiles in the late 1970s. In the future, however, satellite navigation systems will be the most important supplement to INS guidance, even if countries are capable of producing stellar, terrain comparison, or radio update systems. Any country that can build an aircraft or missile INS system should be able to develop an integrated inertial and satellite navigation package providing extremely accurate midcourse guidance. In addition, commercial systems will be widely available for civilian applications.

The United States is developing integrated INS-GPS systems capable of providing missiles with accuracies of less than 20 meters. It might even be possible to attain accuracies of under 5 meters. Even Third World countries should be able to develop systems with accuracies of considerably less than 100 meters, and they might be able to deploy systems with accuracies of under 10 meters.

Inertial Navigation Systems

Until the early 1970s, the only fully developed technology available for cruise missile guidance was an INS package. Inertial guidance uses gyroscopes and accelerometers that detect motion and make possible the calculation of changes in relative position. An important advantage of INS guidance is independence from external support. Unlike other types of guidance, INS devices cannot be jammed or fooled by deceptive countermeasures.

Unfortunately, INS guidance cannot provide high accuracy at long ranges. Gyroscopes are subject to errors that tend to accumulate over time – the longer the flight time, the greater the inaccuracy. Because cruise missiles are relatively slow, they are particularly vulnerable to this gradual loss of accuracy. According to one estimate, U.S. strategic cruise missiles like the Tomahawk are equipped with INS packages giving a drift of 900 meters per hour.[2] In practical terms, this means that a missile with a speed of 800 kilometers per hour that has to fly only 400 kilometers to reach a target is likely to miss by 450 meters. If it flies 1,600 kilometers, it will miss the target by 1,800 meters.

It was the development of small, light-weight, and high-quality INS packages of this type that made possible the production of long-range cruise missiles in the 1970s. Between 1958 and 1970, the accuracy of INS systems improved from 0.03 degrees per hour to 0.005 degrees per hour (or a reduction from about three kilometers of drift per hour to only half a kilometer per hour). Similarly, between 1960 and 1970 it was possible to reduce the weight of missile INS packages from 136 kilograms to only 13 kilograms.[3]

Current commercial standards for INS, defined by civilian aviation authorities, call for a maximum drift of no more than about 1.85 kilometers per hour. Indeed, commercially available navigation systems now are roughly comparable in accuracy and size to the once highly specialized system developed for cruise missile applications. This suggests that Third World countries should have little difficulty acquiring or developing INS packages suitable for use in cruise missiles.

The inherent inaccuracy of INS, however, means that it cannot be the sole guidance system for a highly accurate cruise missile. Additional inputs are needed to correct for INS errors, mandating the use of a hybrid guidance package. The inaccuracy of inertial guidance systems has particularly severe consequences for cruise missiles. A ballistic missile with a range of 600 kilometers requires about 8 minutes to reach its target. In contrast, a cruise missile flying at high subsonic speeds might require 40 minutes to travel the same distance. The difference in flight time becomes even greater as ranges grow. As a result, cruise missiles are more vulnerable than ballistic missiles to inertial drift.

Gyroscopes

The cost of developing and manufacturing a gyroscope increases as its level of accuracy improves. High-quality gyroscopes are difficult to manufacture, and only a relatively small number of companies around the world are capable of producing them. In part, this reflects the limited market for gyroscopes suitable for use in highly accurate INS. The problem becomes especially acute if large numbers are needed.

The technology of gyroscopes has undergone a fundamental revolution during the past 20 years. Mechanical systems have been supplemented by the Ring Laser Gyroscope (RLG), and a Fiber Optic Gyroscope (FOG) is now in an advanced stage of development. An RLG uses mirrors arranged so that a laser light is reflected from one to the next in a continuous loop. Motion causes the laser light to change frequency, making it possible to calculate changes in relative position. A FOG system tracks changing position by detecting minute distortions caused by the motion stresses on the passage of a laser beam through a tightly wound coil of fiber optic cable.

It may be possible to reduce the cost of guidance systems even more. Efforts are now under way to develop integrated INS-GPS guidance systems, suitable for use in high-jamming environments, costing no more than $15,000 and providing accuracies of 20 meters or less. A less demanding design requirement might permit the development of comparable systems for less than $5,000.

A U.S. defense contractor, Northrop, is developing what it calls a micro-optic gyro (MOG), which will be a complete inertial navigation system on a silicon chip. It is expected to cost no more than $1,000 and will make possible the development of extremely small INS packages. Such a system might have a diameter of only 6 centimeters and a width of only 1 centimeter. It will allow a random drift from the true course of 10 degrees per hour. Because this is unacceptably high for weapons covering long ranges, the use of such a system in a cruise missile would require regular position updates from external sources, such as GPS.[4]

Third World Capabilities

Several Third World countries are capable of producing INS systems, including the gyroscopes, although it is not always evident that they have the ability to manufacture the components in large numbers. For example, India makes both rate gyroscopes and accelerometers at the Vikram Sarabhai Space Center (VSSC), and it has demonstrated an ability to develop indigenous INS guidance for its missiles and aircraft.[5] Other Third World countries also are known to produce guidance systems.

Digital Terrain Comparison

TERCOM systems use an on-board radar to map terrain that a missile flies over. In specified areas, the terrain is compared with digitized maps stored in the missile's computer. Matching the two maps makes it possible to determine the precise location of the missile and to correct for navigational errors. Systems of this type were first developed for cruise missiles starting in the late 1940s. The Goodyear Aircraft Corporation began development of the Automatic Terrain Recognition and Navigation (ATRAN) system in 1948. As originally conceived, the system used a radar and radar maps constructed from topographic maps.[6]

A significant advance was reported in the late 1950s with the development of TERCOM. The new system uses a digitized terrain map, consisting of 100- to 3,200-foot cells. A radar altimeter on the missile tracks changes in elevation and compares the inputs to the digitized map. Such systems are reportedly capable of accuracies equal to 0.4 times the size of the smallest cell. This suggests that in theory it is possible to provide accuracies of 40 feet with 100-foot cells. In practice, however, the accuracies are estimated at 100 to 600 feet.[7]

TERCOM became practical only in the early 1970s with the development of small computers. At that time, small, powerful computers were expensive and difficult to build, and the United States was one of the few countries in the world capable of building a practical TERCOM system. This limitation has largely disappeared. Increases in computing power and drastic reductions in cost should make it possible to develop the hardware for TERCOM relatively cheaply. Indeed, it is now possible to purchase extremely inexpensive commercial microprocessors considerably more powerful than the computers used on the Tomahawk and ALCM cruise missiles, which were developed in the 1970s.

Today, the real cost of TERCOM systems is in producing digital maps. To be useful, a TERCOM system must rely on a large, accurate map database. Moreover, these maps have to be updated periodically to compensate for changes in terrain that could affect the functioning of TERCOM. The expense of producing digital maps for use with cruise missiles is so great that the total cost of generating the map databases may approach the investment in missile hardware.

As of 1990, the United States was the only country with operational TERCOM systems, primarily because it was the only country with access to the necessary technology and resources. But a growing number of countries have technical teams that are demonstrating a mastery of the basic techniques. France, Great Britain, Sweden, and Australia all are known to have developed terrain comparison systems, either for manned aircraft or cruise missiles. The British, for example, are planning to retrofit their Tornado GR1 attack aircraft with the SPARTAN navigation system, an integrated guidance package with built-in terrain comparison capabilities.[8]

At least three countries besides the United States appear to have the technology needed to develop missile TERCOM systems. France is producing a TERCOM for its Apache standoff missile with accuracies of 20 meters. It has been reported that Sweden is building a similar system for its proposed Autonomous Standoff Missile (ASOM) glide bomb. And it is generally believed that the Soviet AS-15 and SS-N-21 missiles rely on a TERCOM-like guidance system.[9] India appears to be working on a radar area correlation system for use in ballistic missiles. If it can create a system that is capable of withstanding the stresses of a reentry vehicle, then it will be able to produce one for a cruise missile with relative ease.[10]

Nevertheless, there are reasons to doubt that Third World countries will rely on TERCOM-type systems for cruise missile guidance. The experience of the United States suggests that producing the maps for cruise missiles can be an expensive, complicated process. Some of this experience may be misleading. Digital mapping technology, much of it developed for commercial applications, is now universally available. As increasingly powerful digital computers become more obtainable at ever-decreasing prices, the computational power required for creating digital maps will be accessible to all but the poorest of countries. Equally important, the software needed to generate digital mapping databases is also widely available. At least some Third World countries currently possess digital mapping capabilities.[11] As the production of maps comes to rely more on digital technology, it is inevitable that all countries will possess at least a rudimentary facility to produce digital maps.

Third World countries have considerably smaller geographic areas to map than the United States. More than a decade ago, one source speculated that the United States would need 5,000 different digital maps to support cruise missile operations just against the Soviet Union.[12] Yet the United States anticipates using cruise missiles against countries in the Third World as well. The U.S. Navy, for example, needs digital maps for any part of the world in which it might become engaged. In some cases, this would mean supplying U.S. naval forces with digital maps of targets selected after a ship has gone to sea.

Although Third World countries may choose not to rely on TERCOM-based guidance systems, mission planning for cruise missile strikes may require reliance on digital maps. The United States uses two map databases for planning its cruise missile attacks. The digital terrain elevation database (DTED) provides elevation data, while the vertical obstruction data (VOD) lists obstructions. If Third World countries want to produce cruise missiles capable of flying at low altitudes without incurring the expense of a forward-looking terrain avoidance radar system, digital terrain maps for mission planning will be essential. In this way, a preprogrammed flight path will take into account variations in terrain so that the missile can achieve a low altitude with minimal risk of flying into the ground. A more sophisticated weapon might even incorporate a digital elevation map into the guidance system of the missile itself, thus reducing the time and effort needed to generate the mission instructions for each missile.

Satellite Navigation

Recent developments in satellite navigation techniques are making possible precise navigation at low cost. New constellations of satellites generating navigation signals are largely responsible for the ability of countries in the Third World to develop inexpensive, accurate cruise missiles. The United States and the former Soviet Union are creating competing satellite navigation systems. The United States has devised the Global Positioning System and the Soviets the global navigation satellite system (Glonass). Both countries have navigation satellites in space, but complete constellations will not be in service until the mid-1990s.

The United States developed satellite navigation during the 1960s with the TRANSIT system. Although TRANSIT permitted relatively precise accuracy, it was useful primarily for maritime and land-based applications. The small number of satellites comprising the TRANSIT constellation limited the amount of time during which positional updates could be obtained. As a result, the system was essentially useless for aircraft navigation.

The experience with TRANSIT, however, led the United States to develop a more refined system, the Global Positioning System. The entire GPS network consists of three main elements: ground stations, 24 NAVSTAR satellites, and receivers. The satellites transmit codes that are translated by the receivers into positioning data. The ground stations maintain the accuracy of the system, introducing the minute corrections required on a regular basis. GPS signals are continuously available on a global basis. Ideally, a GPS set would be able to receive signals from 5 satellites at the same time, but until all the satellites are placed in orbit, it will not be possible to provide such coverage for the entire world.[13]

Each NAVSTAR satellite will broadcast two signals. The Coarse/Acquisition signal (C/A code) will be available to any user of the system. The Protected signal (P code) will be encrypted, and only authorized users with the appropriate equipment will be able to access it. The United States intends to encrypt the P code, transforming it into the Y code. The characteristics of the P code are known, so that until the United States starts encrypting the signal it will be possible for anyone to produce receivers that use it. It is estimated that military users of the system will be able to achieve 2- to 15-meter accuracies.[14]

It is believed that Glonass will provide capabilities similar to those of GPS. When fully operational, Glonass will have 24 satellites in service. Each will transmit two separate signals. One set of signals, corresponding to the GPS C/A code, will be openly available. Unlike GPS, every Glonass satellite will broadcast its signal on a different frequency. Glonass satellites also broadcast a separate code, comparable to the GPS P code, that will provide enhanced accuracy for military receivers. As in the case of GPS, it appears that accuracy for civilian users will be about 100 meters in longitude-latitude and 150 meters in altitude.[15] The future of the Glonass system, given the collapse of the Soviet Union, is uncertain.

Cruise missile guidance systems would entail the integration of GPS receivers with more traditional navigation techniques. The GPS modules would provide course updates as part of an inertial navigation system. By replacing existing electronics with more compact integrated circuits, it is possible to incorporate GPS modules into the inertial navigation packages currently in service. It is also possible to use GPS in conjunction with other navigation systems, such as the LORAN-C radionavigation system.[16]

Cost

Only a few years ago, GPS receivers were highly specialized and thus extremely expensive. The U.S. Department of Defense anticipated in 1979 that it would have to pay $116,000 for a five-channel GPS set. Six years later, it bought its first receivers for only $47,000.[17] The cost reduction was a direct result of the growing capabilities and decreasing costs of electronic systems.

The cost of GPS sets has continued to plummet. Typical of the trend is the NavCore V five-channel GPS receiver offered to the commercial market by Rockwell International in early 1991. Designed so that it could be embedded in other systems, the NavCore V was mounted on a 4-by-2.5-inch circuit board. The unit price was $450, although that could drop as low as $225 for quantity purchases.[18]

Current developments will make it possible to incorporate receivers for up to 20 channels at little additional cost over a single-channel receiver. The receivers will be able to track simultaneously as many satellites as they can detect, rather than having to track each satellite in sequence. This will significantly enhance the speed with which position updates can be generated. In the late 1980s, it was believed that such devices could be built for under $4,000 by the mid-1990s.[19] Recent trends suggest that it will not be difficult to exceed this objective.

Cost reductions now make GPS receivers only a small part of the overall price of guidance systems. At the same time, adopting GPS makes it possible to rely on less capable INS packages. When it is possible to update the INS system every second with a new reading from the GPS set, correcting for any drift resulting from gyroscope inaccuracy, high-quality inertial guidance becomes considerably less important.

One implication of integrated INS-GPS packages is

that lower-cost, more easily manufactured INS devices can be used. This can result in significant savings. For example, the U.S. Defense Research Projects Agency is funding the GPS Guidance Package (GGP) program to develop an integrated GPS-FOG inertial guidance system that will provide missile CEPs of less than 20 meters and yet will cost no more than $15,000.[20]

During the first quarter of 1992, several U.S. companies were expected to begin production of GPS chip sets that will further lower costs. According to one estimate, this will make it possible to manufacture a complete GPS package the size of a matchbox for only $150 to $200.[21]

Selective Availability

The destruction of Korean Airline flight KAL 007 by Soviet fighters in 1983 led the United States to reassess its GPS policies. When it was shot down the aircraft was off course, apparently because of a navigation error by the crew. To prevent future incidents of that type, President Ronald Reagan agreed that GPS should be made commercially available.

This presented the Pentagon with a difficult problem. If a civilian user could exploit the inherent accuracy of GPS, so could a potential adversary. Such considerations led to the development of selective availability (S/A). Under selective availability, the U.S. Department of Defense agreed to permit public access to GPS signals but only with an artificially induced reduction in accuracy. Prior to the introduction of selective availability, civilian users relying solely on the C/A code obtained accuracies of between 5 and 30 meters, although accuracies of under 10 meters were common.[22] These data were collected before the entire constellation was available. With selective availability, the accuracy becomes whatever the Department of Defense decides.

It appears that originally the Pentagon promised that implementation of selective availability would provide accuracies of 250 meters at a confidence of 2 dRMS, meaning that at least 95 percent of the time the position reported by GPS would be within 250 meters of the true location. Subsequently, the Pentagon tightened the standard. As of 1991, the guaranteed accuracy was 100 meters with a 2 dRMS confidence. Statistically, a 2 dRMS confidence level equates to a CEP that is four-tenths as large. A 2 dRMS confidence level will include 95 percent of the measurements, whereas a CEP will include only 50 percent of them. This means that a 2 dRMS confidence level of 100 meters is equivalent to a CEP of about 40 meters.[23]

Selective availability will have a substantial impact on the accuracy of the GPS system for users without access to the P code. Because an optimal configuration of satellites will not be visible at all times, it appears that in some parts of the world the accuracies of the system could degenerate to 300 meters.[24]

The implementation of selective availability has been highly controversial. Commercial maritime and aircraft users have fought to preserve access to higher accuracies. Some even have argued that the enhanced accuracies provided by P code signals should be made available to civilian users. The potential benefits are obvious. The full accuracy of GPS is so great that aircraft could rely on it for automated landings under poor weather conditions. In contrast, GPS operating under selective availability provides sufficient accuracy only to navigate a plane as far as the runway approach. Similarly, maritime users have argued that if selective availability were discontinued, it would be possible to use GPS to navigate ships in constricted waters. Nevertheless, the U.S. Department of Defense has rejected all efforts to eliminate selective availability or to allow free access to the encrypted P code portion of GPS signals.[25]

It should be noted, however, that under certain circumstances the degradation may be more apparent than real. The error in the signals is constant within a small geographic region. This means that if GPS indicates that a receiver is 100 meters due north of its true position, it will give the same relative error if the receiver is moved to a new location. As a result, if the true position of the receiver is known before it starts to move, it is possible to calculate the extent of the error and take it into account as the receiver moves from position to position.

Differential GPS

The accuracy of the GPS system can be enhanced through reliance on a system known as differential GPS. This technique requires the use of a ground station, located at a precisely identified location, that broadcasts a correction signal. The additional signal compensates for inaccuracies in the satellite signals.[26] There are several forms of differential GPS. One variety, known as pseudolite, involves using transmitters to generate a signal that is identical in form to the one sent by the satellites, as well as correction data. This has the advantage of total compatibility with standard GPS receivers, but the system works only if the receiver is within about 200 kilometers of the differential transmitter. Moreover, at short ranges the power of the pseudolite transmitter can overwhelm the signals from the satellites.

Another form of differential GPS requires using a correction signal that has been transmitted on a completely different frequency. Careful selection of the frequency can make the corrections useful for receivers located more than 1,000 kilometers from the differential transmitter.[27] This technique requires specialized GPS receivers capable of integrating the two types of signal, which may make the system less reliable and more vulnerable to hostile countermeasures.

Tests of differential GPS have demonstrated significant improvements in accuracy. Even military users with access to the P code can benefit. According to one estimate, differential GPS will make it possible for military users to attain accuracies of between 75 centimeters and 5 meters, rather than the 5- to 15-meter accuracies normally expected. Civilian users may get even more benefit. According to some studies, the accuracy of receivers using only the C/A code can be improved by a factor of 10 through reliance on differential GPS. Preliminary tests suggest that even with the use of selective availability, civilian users can obtain accuracies of 2 to 5 meters.[28]

Ironically, civilian agencies of the U.S. government are responsible for funding the development of differential GPS. The U.S. Coast Guard, National Aeronautics and Space Administration, and the Federal Aviation Administration have sponsored a considerable amount of research related to commercial applications of differential GPS. Recognizing that improvements in GPS accuracy will enhance maritime safety, the Coast Guard reportedly intends to create a network of differential GPS transmitters along the coastline of the United States. Similarly, the Federal Aviation Administration is researching the use of differential GPS as an aircraft landing aid.[29]

Highly automated differential GPS systems are now available on the open market. The cost of commercial differential GPS sets is relatively low, suggesting that most Third World countries would be able to construct one or more stations with little difficulty. As a result, even the poorest countries might have access to the levels of accuracy attained through reliance on differential GPS.

Glonass and INMARSAT

Satellite navigation sets can be built using both GPS and Glonass. This option is likely to attract many Third World countries. By producing systems capable of accessing Glonass as well as GPS, a Third World country could minimize the dangers of such deliberate degradations of accuracy. Receivers that are now being developed for commercial aircraft will be able to exploit signals from both GPS and Glonass satellites.[30]

The ability of the United States to control the accuracy of satellite-generated GPS signals may be reduced by commercial efforts to produce GPS-compatible signals.

INMARSAT, an international group that operates satellites for maritime communications, is currently exploring the addition of GPS transmitters into a proposed new generation of satellites. Current plans call for four satellites, which will be placed in geosynchronous orbit. These satellites will provide global coverage, ensuring that every part of the world is within the area of coverage of at least one INMARSAT satellite. Some areas, such as Western Europe, will be covered by three satellites. This means that every GPS receiver will automatically gain access to at least one additional GPS satellite. The simple availability of from one to three additional satellites will automatically increase the potential accuracy of the GPS system.[31]

Other proposed features of INMARSAT should further enhance the accuracy of the system. This "GPS Overlay" will include updated information on the health of the GPS constellation, indicating which satellites are known to be generating inaccurate information and perhaps providing corrective data.[32]

It is not yet known how much the INMARSAT constellation would improve GPS receivers using the C/A code under selective availability. Preliminary studies, however, suggest that a geosynchronous satellite providing corrective data might compensate in large measure for the errors introduced by selective availability, possibly permitting accuracies of less than 10 meters.[33]

Alternatives to GPS

Several U.S. companies are designing satellite systems that would provide some of the same capabilities as GPS. Although intended primarily for communications, the systems would generate positioning data as well. The systems now under consideration would consist of a constellation of small, inexpensive satellites placed into low earth orbit. Reductions in the cost and size of electronic components has made it possible to build so-called light satellites that weigh only 100 to 200 kilograms. Consequently, the cost of such systems should be relatively small.[34] One company has calculated that for only $650 million it could place in service a constellation of 24 small satellites providing global communications and positioning services.

According to one estimate, it might be possible to achieve accuracies of 15 to 20 meters with these systems.[35] Thus, satellite navigation systems that are totally independent of the existing GPS and Glonass systems could become available during the 1990s. This means that Third World countries interested in using satellite navigation for cruise missiles may have access to systems providing redundancy and enhancing perceived reliability.

GPS and the Third World

Third World countries are aware of the potential value of satellite navigation systems. Israel is developing a GPS navigation system for unmanned aerial vehicles. A subsidiary of Israel Aircraft Industries, Tamam, has completed development of the TR90 strapdown inertial navigation platform. It is now working on a new program, a modular integrated GPS-IN system. The Delilah unmanned air vehicle is now equipped with a GPS package providing positioning accuracy of "better than 91 meters." Israel has shown a willingness to export such technology. In early 1990, for example, it agreed to supply Chile with integrated INS-GPS packages to upgrade F-5E fighter aircraft.[36]

South Africa is working on GPS systems for military applications. An airborne unit is now under development, and a simpler system designed for maritime operations was expected to become operational in 1990. Indian scientists have expressed an interest in the possible use of GPS receivers to provide midcourse guidance correction for ballistic missile reentry vehicles.[37] If India was able to produce a system suitable for use with a ballistic missile, it should have little difficulty developing one for the less demanding conditions faced by cruise missiles.

At present, Third World countries confront few problems in acquiring GPS sets. GPS packages using only C/A codes are available even for military applications. For example, the United States supplied Egypt with a GPS system capable of locating the position of a mini-RPV with an accuracy of approximately 60 meters.[38] Other countries may be able to acquire the technology needed to produce GPS systems, including Brazil, Singapore, South Korea, and Taiwan. This suggests that GPS-INS technology suitable for long-range cruise missiles will become widely available in the Third World during the early 1990s.

Both the United States and the former Soviet Union are trying to limit the accuracy of the satellite navigation data made available to civilian users. In theory, selective availability will prevent Third World military forces from using GPS to deliver ordnance with an accuracy better than about 100 meters. For some applications, that may be enough. No country in the Third World is likely to desire greater accuracy for the delivery of strategic weapons. When attacking an area target, such as a city or a large equipment storage site, accuracies of 100 meters may be sufficient, especially if large numbers of cheap weapons can be used. Certainly Iran and Iraq would have been content if the conventionally armed ballistic missiles fired during their 1980–1988 conflict had struck within 100 meters of the target.

Terminal Guidance

During the mid-1990s, the United States will become able to deliver aircraft weapons with considerable accuracy, partly by using extremely cheap satellite navigation systems. Air-delivered munitions will be delivered with accuracies of 10 meters, even without relying on sophisticated guidance systems.[39] GPS systems, especially if employed with differential techniques, may be able to provide accuracies of 5 meters or less.

In many cases, however, more precision may be required. To destroy a particular building or to hit a specific part of that building, accuracies of less than five meters may be necessary. The conventionally armed cruise missiles developed by the United States and France draw on several guidance techniques to enhance missile accuracy. It is unlikely that all of their methods will be of interest to Third World countries, but some may be adopted directly.

The U.S. Navy's SLAM missile uses a GPS-INS guidance system that is tied to a Maverick IIR seeker and a Walleye II data link. With this system, the GPS package navigates the missile to the vicinity of the target, and the weapons officer on the launching aircraft (many kilometers away) selects the target that the IIR seeker will home in on.[40] The United States has a terminal guidance technique for cruise missiles, known as a Digital Scene Matching Area Correlator (DSMAC), that reportedly produces a CEP of between one and three meters. The French are known to be building a similar terminal guidance system into their Apache missile. Using a millimeter wave radar, the system is capable of achieving accuracies of about one meter.[41]

Third World countries are likely to be least attracted to DSMAC systems or the French equivalent. But India's interest in developing a radar area correlation system for ballistic missile reentry vehicles suggests that it may wish to build such systems for cruise missiles.[42]

More interesting is the system used on the SLAM, as it employs readily accessible, proven technologies. Israel is known to have advanced guidance systems, some of which might be suitable for use in land attack cruise missiles. Israel and Iraq are among the Third World countries known to have developed terminal guidance technologies that could be used with cruise missiles.

Israel, for example, has developed several precision-guided munitions. The Popeye air-to-surface standoff missile uses a television-guidance package with a data link, allowing a human operator to direct the missile during its last minute of flight. This weapon, now in service with the Israeli Air Force and the U.S. Strategic Air Command, is rocket-propelled and has a reported range of 90 to 100 kilometers. The Opher terminal guidance bomb kit converts ordinary "iron" bombs into guided glide bombs. The Opher is carried and delivered as if it were an ordinary dumb bomb. When the bomb is 1,000 meters from the target, its infrared homing seeker locks onto the heat of the target and the trajectory of the bomb is corrected to ensure a direct hit. Finally, the Pyramid television-guided glide bomb has a standoff range of up to 30 kilometers. The bomb weighs 360 kilograms and apparently consists of a modified 500-pound Mk 82 bomb fitted with an electro-optical guidance system and a data link. The system is reported to have a CEP of only one meter.[43]

In 1989, Iraq claimed to have developed two precision-guided weapons. The first was the Saquar infrared-guided glide bomb, with a range of eight kilometers. It used a heat-seeking guidance system to autonomously track the target once the bomb was released.[44] The second was a kit to convert 1,000-pound Mk 84 bombs into television-guided weapons. Here, a Japanese television camera was mounted in the nose of the weapon, and the bomb could be controlled from either the ground or the air. The system was expected to enter service in late 1989.[45]

Other Third World countries can build similar types of terminal guidance systems. By the early 1980s both South Africa and Taiwan were producing television-guidance mechanisms for their versions of the Gabriel 2 antiship missile. This suggests that they may be able to produce more sophisticated systems today.

A question mark surrounds possible applications of the Global Positioning System for terminal guidance. Some reports indicate that differential GPS systems could provide positioning data with an accuracy of three to five meters. If this proves to be the case, and if it is possible to develop weapons guidance systems that can take advantage of such precise data, then it also might be possible to cheaply build terminally guided cruise missiles with an accuracy of three to five meters.

Conclusion

The availability of satellite navigation systems will make it possible to produce highly accurate, inexpensive cruise missile guidance systems. Indeed, adoption of differential GPS should allow Third World countries to develop guidance systems with accuracies of 10 meters or less. Few countries will rely solely on GPS, because it would make them vulnerable to changes in U.S. policy. Use of integrated GPS-Glonass receivers and reliance on a GPS Overlay such as the proposed INMARSAT system would significantly reduce dependence on GPS alone.

Terminal guidance will pose a more serious problem. It is highly unlikely, however, that any Third World country will be able to acquire DSMAC-type systems. In contrast, a considerable number of countries may be able to acquire man-in-the-loop systems such as those used with the U.S. Navy's SLAM. Certain types of special-purpose terminal guidance also might be obtainable. For example, it should not be difficult to acquire infrared or radar seekers for anti-ship attacks. Antiradiation seekers also may be available. But only a few countries are likely to obtain land attack homing systems for use against armored vehicles, such as those being developed for the German KDAR.

If it is possible to develop satellite navigation systems with accuracies of three meters, the problem of terminal guidance will be largely solved. Simply by using a satellite navigation system a country could deliver ordnance with an accuracy comparable to that of most existing precision-guided munitions. It is not yet clear, however, whether it will be possible to build weapons that can take advantage of the theoretical possibilities provided by satellite navigation. Highly accurate satellite navigation systems would enable Third World countries to develop a range of tactical and strategic weapons capable of hitting point targets. This would provide levels of accuracy not currently available to most Third World countries.

5

Building Cruise Missiles

The technologies needed to design and manufacture cruise missiles have become widely available in the Third World countries. Some countries are already producing cruise missiles, usually antiship weapons. An increasing number of nations in the Third World build combat aircraft and remotely piloted vehicles, indicating that they have access to the basic production skills needed to manufacture cruise missiles.

Many Third World countries appear capable of designing indigenous systems, even if they remain dependent on technology and components acquired from industrialized countries. The indigenous development and manufacture of cruise missiles require expertise in airframes, propulsion systems, flight controls, and warheads. As important as the design and production of components, however, is the ability to integrate them into a completed system. Even the United States has experienced difficulties with such integration.[1]

Several Third World countries already have a demonstrated ability to design and produce cruise missiles. Israel, South Africa, and Taiwan have designed indigenous antiship cruise missiles, and Brazil and India appear to be doing the same. Iraq and North Korea can assemble ASCMs; Iraq also may be able to introduce modifications into the basic design.

Other countries may have the capacity to produce cruise missiles during the 1990s, although it is impossible to predict exactly which ones will have the requirements, resources, and technical skills. Examination of existing aerospace and defense industries in the Third World, however, can define more clearly the extent to which certain countries might be capable of initiating production. This involves looking at the potential of countries to produce cruise missile airframes by surveying the manufacture of aircraft and remotely piloted vehicles, as well as examining engine production and warhead fabrication capabilities.

Airframes

A cruise missile is an expendable remotely piloted vehicle or a small unmanned airplane. This suggests that any country capable of producing either RPVs or combat aircraft should be able to manufacture cruise missiles as well. At least 15 Third World countries currently manufacture either combat aircraft or RPVs or are in the process of establishing production programs. It is possible that additional countries will create the infrastructure needed to develop or manufacture such systems during the 1990s.

The level of design and manufacturing expertise varies considerably from one country to another. Some of these nations have sophisticated capabilities, allowing them to produce systems comparable in quality to those built in the industrialized countries. But even nations with the indigenous technical base needed to produce cruise missiles rely on foreign technology. Others are totally dependent on foreign assistance and often can do little more than assemble systems that use only a few indigenously produced components.

Remotely Piloted Vehicles

At least 10 Third World countries – Argentina, Brazil, India, Indonesia, Iran, Iraq, Israel, Saudi Arabia, South Africa, and South Korea – are thought to be making RPVs.[2] The level of sophistication varies, however, and production capabilities appear to be quite rudimentary in some cases. For example, countries like Indonesia and Saudi Arabia produce only simple mini-RPVs, which are little more than large model aircraft. Other nations, such as Israel and South Africa, are capable of developing relatively sophisticated RPVs. A number of countries, like South Korea, have embarked on development programs that could enable them to build reasonably sophisticated RPVs.

The link between RPVs and cruise missiles is strong. Argentina and Iraq, for instance, have converted RPVs into cruise missiles. Both countries manufacture licensed versions of the Mirach 100 RPV, which was developed in Italy by Meteor. Although these were intended primarily for reconnaissance missions, Meteor designed variants that can operate as land attack cruise missiles.

During the 1980s, Argentina developed the MQ-2 Bigua, a version of the Mirach 100. The Bigua has multiple roles. Reportedly, it has the capability to operate as a reconnaissance platform, decoy, electronic warfare system, and attack weapon and can be altered to attack either ships or land targets. The Bigua can be launched from a ramp if a rocket booster is attached, or it can be released from a helicopter or an Argentine-built IA 58 Pucara attack aircraft. It is not known whether a terminal guidance system is available for use with the Bigua.[3]

Iraq also bought Mirach 100 remotely piloted vehicles during the 1980s for use in reconnaissance missions and produced at least a few copies under license. In May 1989, Iraq displayed a cruise missile, called the Ababil, which apparently was based on a larger, more capable RPV, the Mirach 600. Although Meteor initiated design of the Mirach 600s in the mid-1980s, it is not known to have built any prototypes. Published descriptions indicate that the Mirach 600 was supposed to weigh a maximum of 1,000 kilograms while carrying a combat load of 300 to 500 kilograms. Range was not specified, but it was expected to have an endurance of two hours while flying at speeds of up to Mach 0.92. The Mirach 600 uses the same automatic navigation system fitted to the Mirach 100.[4]

The transformation of RPVs into cruise missiles is not a recent invention of Third World countries. During the 1960s, the Swedish Navy developed the Rb 08A antiship missile based on the French CT.20 turbojet-powered target drone. The CT.20 also was produced in reconnaissance versions. As an antiship missile, the Rb 08A has a range of 250 kilometers with a 250-kilogram warhead. The Soviet Union apparently went in the opposite direction and acquired several RPVs based on cruise missiles. According to some reports, it had RPV versions of the SS-N-3 Shaddock/SSC-1 Sepal family of ASCMs. In addition, the Soviets adopted the SS-N-12 Sandbox ship-launched antiship missile as an RPV.[5]

Other Third World countries may be developing cruise missiles based on RPV designs. Iranian officials claimed that they could fit warheads to three small mini-RPVs that were displayed in May 1989. Similarly, the Indian PTA, ostensibly a target drone, has an admitted attack capability.[6]

Aircraft Industries

A growing number of Third World nations are capable of producing military aircraft. Countries currently manufacturing military aircraft, or with plans to do so, include Argentina, Brazil, Egypt, India, Indonesia, Israel, North Korea, South Africa, South Korea, and Taiwan. Others, such as Chile and Singapore, have some ability to modernize combat aircraft. Although transport and training aircraft are the most common products of Third World aircraft industries, at least six of these countries have supersonic fighter programs. Moreover, some of them are substantial producers of aircraft. Brazil, for example, became the world's sixth largest manufacturer of aircraft in the late 1980s.[7] Although all of these countries depend on foreign technology to some extent, even the ability to assemble fighters demonstrates considerable production skill.

At least six Third World countries manufacture supersonic aircraft. India has assembled several Soviet fighters, including the MiG-21 and the MiG-29, and it is now attempting to design an indigenous fighter, the LCA. Israel designed and manufactured the Kfir, a version of the French Mirage 5 fighter. It also designed and built the Lavi fighter, although financial pressures led to cancellation of the program. North Korea is believed to make a version of the Soviet MiG-21, although this may amount to little more than the assembly of components acquired in China. South Korea has assembled F-5 fighters and plans to build the FSX, a derivative of the U.S. F-16. South Africa has assembled French Mirage F-1 fighters and has established a program to produce the CAVA fighter. Taiwan is receiving extensive assistance from the United States in its efforts to develop its IDF fighter.

Other Third World countries have manufactured aircraft capable of undertaking both light attack and training roles. Argentina has made the IA 58A Pucara, a turboprop-powered light aircraft and has developed–with German assistance–the IA 63 Pampa. Brazil is collaborating with Italy to produce the AMX. Chile has assembled a version of the Spanish CASA C-101, and Egypt has put together copies of the Franco-German Alpha Jet. In addition, countries like Singapore have relatively competent aviation industries that cannot build aircraft but possess sophisticated overhaul and rebuild capabilities. Countries with such expertise might be able to manufacture cruise missiles.

Advanced Materials

At least some Third World countries are acquiring the technologies needed to produce more sophisticated airframes.

Some developing countries may be able to incorporate stealthlike technologies in their missiles. According to the director of naval intelligence, as of early 1991 "almost 40 countries have expressed interest in obtaining LO [low-observable] technology or systems." A year earlier, the same official gave a lower estimate but noted the growing availability of stealthy technologies:

> Only a few industrialized countries can incorporate the more sophisticated aspects of stealth technology into their weapon systems. Commercially available radar absorbing materials and associated testing ranges are, however, more common. This presages the time when numerous countries will be able to reduce the detectability of their missiles, as well as other major weapon platforms. We must deal with no less than 17 countries exploiting this relatively new field, and the number is likely to grow rapidly.[8]

In 1991, U.S. officials identified nine industrialized countries known to be exploiting low-observable technology: Australia, Canada, France, Germany, Great Britain, Italy, the former Soviet Union, Sweden, and the United States.[9] Although none of these countries is in the Third World, the length of the list illustrates the spread of the technology. This suggests that at least some Third World states should be able to work with low-observable technology, either through indigenous development or by acquisition from one of the industrialized countries.

A considerable number of Third World countries are known to have developed some capability to utilize composite materials that reduce missile radar observability. Countries like India, Israel, South Africa, South Korea, and Taiwan have demonstrated systems that incorporate composite materials.[10] Some Third World missiles make extensive use of them. Reportedly, more than 40 percent of the structure of Taiwan's Hsiung Feng II missile will be made from composite materials.[11]

The availability of low-observable technology is important for the design of survivable cruise missiles. A cruise missile capable of surviving modern air defenses needs to minimize visibility. It must be small in size and should be constructed from materials that reduce the radar signature of the system. It is possible that access to composite materials may be helpful in the construction of missile airframes and components.

Although the United States has taken the lead in the design of stealthy cruise missiles, other countries have some capability as well. OTO Melara, the Italian company that produces the OTOMAT antiship missile, is working on versions of the OTOMAT that will use low-observable technology. Similarly, the French ASLP strategic cruise missile will incorporate stealth techniques to reduce radar cross section.[12] The adoption of stealth technology by European countries suggests that it also may become available to Third World countries during the 1990s.

Propulsion Systems and Flight Controls

No one type of engine is unique to cruise missiles. Strictly defined, a cruise missile has an air-breathing engine. This study uses a looser definition, however, accepting that some rocket-powered weapons also can be called cruise missiles. Most rocket-powered cruise missiles fall into one of two categories. First, there are antiship missiles, such as the French Exocet or the Soviet Styx, which have been built by Iraq, Israel, North Korea, South Africa, and Taiwan. These weapons could be turned into simple land attack missiles. In the second category are air-launched, rocket-powered land attack weapons, such as the U.S. AGM-130 (maximum range, 48 kilometers). Rocket-powered weapons of this type are essentially powered gliders that have been built around a standard aircraft bomb and fitted with a terminal guidance system—usually either a laser or electro-optical guidance system. Israel, which manufactures the Popeye, a rocket-powered weapon adopted by the U.S. Air Force as the Have Nap, is the only Third World country known to build such weapons. As unpowered glide weapons become more effective, many rocket-powered weapons are expected to disappear. It is now possible to produce glide bombs with ranges of at least 30 kilometers.[13]

To achieve long ranges, however, requires air-breathing engines. Third World countries will not need engines as sophisticated as those now built in the United States. In most cases, they can rely on simple turbojet engines comparable to those manufactured in the United States 20 years ago, such as the J402 used on the U.S. Harpoon missile. More complex engines, like the turbofan F-107, will be required only for the development of a small, long-range missile that is comparable in range and payload to the ALCM or the Tomahawk.

Engines designed for cruise missiles are built in many countries besides the United States, including the former Soviet Union, China, France, and Great Britain. During the 1980s, French and British manufacturers of engines showed a willingness to supply Third World customers. Although China is not known to have exported its expendable turbojet engines, its support for Third World ballistic missile programs suggests that it also would be willing to assist cruise missile projects.[14]

Two French companies make cruise missile engines, Microturbo and Societe Turbomeca. Microturbo engines are used in missiles as diverse as the Swedish RBS15 antiship missile, the British Sea Eagle, the French Apache, and the Mirach family of remotely piloted vehicles. Significantly, Microturbo appears to have supplied engines to countries, like Argentina and Iraq, that were involved in the development of cruise missiles. India used the TRI 60 engine in early versions of its PTA drone project. Societe Turbomeca produces engines used in the Italian OTOMAT and the Taiwanese Hsiung Feng II antiship missiles. Taiwan was given a license to produce the Arbizon 4 engine used in the Hsiung Feng II.[15]

The British company Noel Penny Turbines produces an assortment of engines, some suitable for use in mini-RPVs and others with enough thrust to power a large cruise missile. According to one source, this firm supplied the engine used in the Israeli Delilah harassment drone. China produces the Wopen turbojet engine, which was first used on the air-launched C 802 antiship missile.[16]

The level of technology that exists in the Third World is evident from the number of countries able to build jet engines for supersonic fighters. India, Israel, South Africa, and Taiwan currently have fighter engine manufacturing capabilities.[17] Other countries can make less sophisticated types of turbojet engines.[18] Such countries probably possess the basic technology needed to produce small turbojets.

Information on small engine development in the Third World is scanty, but enough is known to indicate that several countries – India, Israel, South Africa, and Taiwan – can manufacture small turbojet engines comparable to the U.S. J402. Third World countries should have little difficulty obtaining the small engines used in harassment drones, which typically might be only 25-horsepower engines. India has developed a small turbojet engine for its Pilotless Target Aircraft (PTA). The PTAE-7, which is being developed by Hindustan Aeronautics, will generate 350 kilograms of thrust.[19] If successful, this program will provide India with the technology needed to produce an expendable engine for cruise missiles.

Israel is known to have small engines suitable for use in small cruise missiles. Bet-Shemesh Engines designed the Sorek 4 expendable engine for "cruise missiles, RPVs and long duration drones." The engine underwent bench testing starting in June 1982 and entered production that summer.[20] It is not known whether this is the same engine used in the new Gabriel 4 antiship missile. Other Israeli companies also are reported to be doing work on engines suitable for use in cruise missiles. For example, Israel Military Industries may be conducting research and development in air-breathing propulsion, including scramjets, ramjets, and small turbojets.[21]

South Africa has developed a "low-cost expendable gas turbine engine," which has been under production "since the early eighties." This engine, the APA-1, is capable of generating thrust of 336 kilograms; it can operate at speeds of up to Mach 0.9 and at altitudes of up to 33,000 feet. This missile may also be used in an over-the-horizon antiship missile tested by South Africa in 1989.[22]

Taiwan is believed to produce a license-built version of the Turbomeca's Arbizon IV engine for the Hsiung Feng II antiship missile.[23] The Arbizon IV engine generates 337 kilograms thrust and weighs only 60 kilograms. Other countries possess more rudimentary capabilities. Reportedly, in the early 1980s Brazil developed a small turbojet engine for remotely piloted vehicles. Known as the PMO/CBT Tiete, this engine produced a thrust of only 31 kilograms. It was developed by the Mechanical Division (PMO-Divisao de Mechanica) of the Aerospace Technical Institute (CTA). The engine was used on a Brazilian mini-RPV first flown in 1983.[24]

In addition to the four Third World countries currently capable of producing engines for small, short-range cruise missiles, others are likely to be added to this total during the 1990s. It is significant, however, that all known engine programs are for turbojet engines rather than for the more efficient turbofan engines. This suggests that it may be some time before small long-range cruise missiles appear in the Third World.

With the growing number of turbojet engine producers, it appears that even Third World countries unable to make turbojet engines should be able to acquire them. If industrialized countries are reluctant to sell suitable engines, China or Third World countries with expertise in turbojet production may be willing to supply them. As a result, even the absence of an indigenous engine production capability may not prevent a country from building a cruise missile.

Warheads

Cruise missiles can be armed with a variety of different warheads, depending on the mission of the weapon. Antiship and antiradiation missiles typically have high-explosive warheads. Cruise missile warheads also can be fitted with conventional cluster munitions, fuel air explosives, chemical agents, biological agents, or nuclear devices.

No Third World country is known to possess a cruise missile delivery capability for nuclear weapons. Moreover, it is unclear whether any nation in the Third World would adopt cruise missiles as the primary means for delivering nuclear weapons. Because a nuclear warhead would experience less stress on a cruise missile than on a ballistic missile, given the differences in the velocity and acceleration of the two types of missiles, it might be easier to construct such a warhead for a cruise missile. On the other hand, because cruise missiles are slower than ballistic missiles and are potentially more vulnerable to air defenses, they could be viewed as less reliable.

Cruise missiles make an excellent delivery system for chemical and biological weapons. It is possible to fit cruise missiles with spray tanks, a relatively simple technology for releasing chemical and biological agents, that should be available to most Third World countries. There is no evidence, however, that any Third World country has attempted to develop a biological or chemical delivery system for cruise missiles.

The potential accuracy of cruise missiles may make even conventionally armed cruise missiles highly attractive to Third World countries. It appears that subsonic cruise missiles can be armed with munitions similar to those delivered by aircraft. The trajectory and speeds encountered by a cruise missile are roughly comparable to those of an aircraft. Thus, it should be possible for Third World countries to adapt technologies associated with aircraft bombs in the manufacture of cruise missile warheads.

High-explosive warheads can be developed relatively easily. The United States has fitted several missiles, including the SLAM, the TASM, and the TLAM-C, with the same 450-kilogram warhead originally developed for the Bullpup air-to-surface missile.[25] But the new Block III versions of the TLAM-C will rely on an improved 320-kilogram warhead that is claimed to have equal destructive effects.[26] That it is possible to reduce warhead weight by 30 percent and yet not diminish the effectiveness of the weapon suggests that it is important to pay as much attention to improvements in the design of a high-explosive warhead as to its actual weight.

A Third World country might be able to acquire specialized submunitions for a cruise missile warhead from an existing producer of submunitions. Because cluster munition weapons are exported widely, it may be possible for a nation to acquire even sophisticated submunitions, such as the SG357 runway cratering submunitions and the HB876 area denial mines used in the British JP233 air base attack bomb. Even if the British were unwilling to supply the submunitions for a cruise missile warhead, it might be possible for Third World countries to acquire bombs intended for aircraft delivery and then use the submunitions in a cruise missile.

A considerable number of countries in the Third World are capable of making cluster munition warheads. Countries known to produce cluster munition delivery systems — for either artillery ammunition, aircraft-delivered bombs, rocket warheads, or missile warheads — include Brazil, Chile, Egypt, India, Iraq, Israel, South Africa, and South Korea.[27] Some of these cluster bombs are rather sophisticated. Cardoen, a Chilean arms manufacturer that works closely with South Africa and Iraq, has produced the CB-770, a cluster bomb area denial system. Intended for deployment against air bases, the CB-770 carries 121 PM3 bomblets, which are delayed-action submunitions. The bomblets, which weigh 2.2 kilograms, can be timed to explode from 30 seconds to 72 hours after delivery. A single 400-kilogram CB-770 bomb can cover an area of up to 50,000 square meters.[28]

A number of Third World countries are known to be working on fuel air explosives (FAEs). An FAE creates a cloud of explosive gas. When the cloud is detonated, it produces a powerful blast. Among those believed to have the technology are Argentina, Chile, India, Iraq, and Israel.

Several of these countries are known to be working on FAEs for missile and rocket warheads.[29] Cruise missiles provide an excellent delivery system for FAEs; in important respects they are superior to ballistic missiles. An FAE munition needs to be moving relatively slowly when the gas cloud is created. This is considerably easier to achieve if the munition is delivered from a subsonic cruise missile than it would be from a ballistic missile reentry vehicle traveling at supersonic speeds.

Conclusion

At least 10 and possibly as many as 15 Third World countries might be able to produce cruise missiles during the 1990s. Not all of these countries have the capability to develop all of the elements that go into the production of cruise missiles. But by relying on foreign assistance, even the countries with limited expertise might be able to build cruise missile systems.

A considerable number of these countries possess the skill to manufacture cruise missile airframes. Countries currently without such skills could probably acquire the capability with few problems. This is unlikely to be a constraint on Third World production of cruise missiles. The sophistication of the airframes will vary considerably from one country to another, however. Several nations may be able to exploit low-observable technology for cruise missile designs, but others will be capable of producing little more than simple airframes based on foreign designs.

Engines suitable for cruise missiles are now available in the Third World. Several countries manufacture small turbojet engines, and others probably are technically able to produce them. Even countries that currently do not have the capacity to make suitable engines could probably obtain them from foreign sources. In addition, Third World countries may become a potential source of engines, given the apparent ability of India, Israel, South Africa, and Taiwan to manufacture small turbojet engines.

A large number of Third World countries have expertise in the development and production of warheads, including some of sophisticated design. Countries known to have worked with cluster munition warheads include Brazil, Chile, Egypt, India, Iraq, Israel, and South Africa. Some of these countries have devised warheads for use in ballistic missiles and others for use in air-launched glide bombs.

Until recently, guidance was a major obstacle to the production of cruise missiles. For land attack, TERCOM systems were needed, and no Third World country was likely to acquire them. The arrival of the Global Positioning System, however, has enabled Third World countries to manufacture long-range systems with considerable accuracy. As a result, it will be possible for nations in the Third World to build guidance packages to provide missiles with accuracies of 100 meters or less. Relying on differential GPS, they may be able to build short-range systems with accuracies of 5 meters.

There is little evidence that Third World countries will have the capability to produce sophisticated terminal guidance systems. When attacking point targets, missiles must achieve accuracies of less than 10 meters. Given the availability of seekers for antiship and antiradiation missiles, at least some countries should be able to make such systems. For weapons with relatively short ranges, a solution like SLAM is a possibility. Several countries appear to have the ability to produce video-guidance packages for missiles, including Israel, South Africa, and Taiwan.

For systems with longer ranges, a totally autonomous system would be needed. Although this technology might become available to Third World arms industries, it is uncertain that many Third World countries would be able to afford such a costly system.

6

Responses to Cruise Missile Proliferation

It seems clear that the proliferation of cruise missiles will become a growing concern in the 1990s. This suggests that efforts to constrain the spread of these weapons, and to cope with them once they have proliferated, will receive increasing attention. Although this chapter concentrates on U.S. responses to the problem, much of the discussion will necessarily have a broader focus. Many of the policy options available to the United States require the involvement of other countries. The Missile Technology Control Regime is effective only because it is multilateral in character, and arms control agreements by their nature require more than one participant.

U.S. Policy

The proliferation of cruise missiles poses a potentially serious threat to the interests of the United States.[1] Hostile countries that acquire long-range, highly accurate cruise missiles will have the capability to attack targets that are important to the United States and its allies. Even conventionally armed missiles that rely on satellite navigation systems might have sufficient accuracy to inflict significant damage to critical military and civilian installations.

Although not generally recognized, the United States is now implementing policies intended to prevent the proliferation of some types of cruise missiles. To tackle the problem, it has adopted three separate approaches. First, since the early 1980s U.S. officials have promoted the use of multilateral controls to limit the export of cruise missiles and related technologies. As an original party to the MTCR, the United States is now working with other countries to stop the further spread of cruise missiles capable of carrying a 500-kilogram payload to a range of at least 300 kilometers.

Second, since the late 1980s the United States has paid increasing attention to arms control initiatives. For example, the Bush administration has supported arms control agreements to ban all surface-to-surface missiles, including cruise missiles, in the Middle East. This approach has been accepted in principle by the four other permanent members of the United Nations Security Council.

Finally, the U.S. military is developing defenses against cruise missiles. The effectiveness of these defenses is uncertain, as existing air defense systems against modern cruise missiles have never been tested in battle. Thus, we do not yet know whether the country's current systems, which may have the technical characteristics to defeat cruise missiles, will be able to do so in practice.

These three approaches are not mutually exclusive. Indeed, they are really complementary. Export controls and arms control agreements can make defenses more effective by constraining the potential threat. Similarly, the existence of effective defenses can reduce the attractiveness of cruise missiles and thus make arms control agreements more likely.

Yet the United States is not against the spread of all cruise missiles. The Missile Technology Control Regime does not capture all types of cruise missile systems, and arms control agreements ignore many types of cruise missiles. Indeed, the United States promotes the export of short-range antiship cruise missiles, such as the Harpoon. Similarly, it condones the efforts of friendly countries to develop certain kinds of cruise missiles, such as the Israeli Harpy harassment drone. Nor does the United States prohibit the export of cruise missile technologies for use in other types of systems, such as remotely piloted vehicles. In support of this objective, the government permits the export of many technologies that could be used to develop cruise missiles. Thus, U.S. policy opposes only cruise missiles that conflict with the MTCR guidelines.

In addition, the United States does not oppose the transfer of every technology that could be used in the development of cruise missiles. Many of these technologies have legitimate civilian uses, and for this reason the focus of U.S. policy is to ensure that such technologies are not illicitly diverted to military applications. As a result, there is an inevitable tension between those activities that the United States seeks to prevent and those it condones.

Israel provides a good example of a country that has become dependent on cruise missiles and other systems that use similar technologies. Its navy was one of the first to rely on antiship cruise missiles for surface combat capabilities. Since the early 1970s, Israeli intelligence has assigned a high priority to remotely piloted vehicles. The country has been a pioneer in the development of mini-RPVs. Harassment drones and decoys have a central role in efforts by the Israeli Air Force to defeat hostile air defenses. Finally, it appears that the Israeli military believes that kamikaze drones and standoff munitions are essential to maintain its qualitative superiority.[2] Israel is not unique. Other friends and allies of the United States have a similar dependence on cruise missile technology.

The result of U.S. policy is an ambivalence that reflects an important reality: cruise missiles, and systems that use cruise missile technology, play an increasingly significant role in the military forces of countries friendly to the United States. Thus, an attempt by the United States to prevent its allies from acquiring antiship cruise missiles and remotely piloted vehicles would undermine the security of friendly nations.

Threats to the United States

With their increasing proliferation, cruise missiles will present a considerable challenge to the United States. For the near term, they will be a threat primarily to U.S. friends and allies and to U.S. military forces deployed overseas. Except for the former Soviet Union, no military force possesses cruise missiles capable of attacking the continental United States.

By the end of the 1990s, however, cruise missiles capable of attacking the continental United States could appear in the inventories of some countries. At present, no Third World country can produce a strategic bomber, and it is unlikely that any Third World country will be able to develop such a weapon.[3] Nor does it appear that any Third World country will be able to develop an intercontinental ballistic missile during the next decade. Indeed, the CIA estimated that only three Third World countries are expected to possess ballistic missiles with ranges of more than 3,000 kilometers by the end of the century.[4] Consequently, ballistic missiles and manned aircraft will pose only a limited threat to the territory of the United States during the 1990s.

In contrast, it is possible that Third World countries could acquire cruise missiles capable of striking the United States. Cruise missiles can be launched from ships and aircraft. Thus, even without possessing intercontinental cruise missiles, nations in the Third World might be able to deploy platforms carrying cruise missiles within range of U.S. territory.

Third World countries should have little difficulty developing long-range cruise missiles, although at present there is no indication that any of these nations intends to develop cruise missiles with the range of U.S. and Soviet strategic cruise missiles. A Third World country possessing a cruise missile similar to the French Apache would have a potential range of as much as 1,000 kilometers.

What can be accomplished, even with old technology, is shown by the strategic cruise missiles developed by the

United States during the 1950s. Any Third World country capable of developing and building supersonic fighter aircraft ought to be able to emulate, or significantly improve upon, those designs. For example, the U.S. Air Force Snark missile, a turbojet-powered, ground-launched cruise missile could travel 8,000 kilometers while carrying a 3,200-kilometer payload. Similarly, the U.S. Navy Regulus II, a turbojet-powered, ship-launched cruise missile, had a range of more than 2,000 kilometers with a 1,300-kilometer warhead, although the range dropped to only 1,050 kilometers when the missile flew at Mach 2.[5] Although these weapons were unsuccessful at the time, many of the problems that beset them were resolved in more modern weapons.

Consider, for example, the characteristics of a missile like the Regulus II. It was built with J79 turbojet engines, which are also used in aircraft like the F-4E Phantom II and the F-104 Starfighter. Large quantities of surplus J79 engines have become available because many of the aircraft using the engine have been removed from service. Moreover, at least one Third World country – Israel – has even manufactured the J79. Similar engines are made in other Third World countries, including India and South Africa. Hence, the type of engine used in the Regulus missile is now easily obtained.

There is no reason to believe, however, that Third World countries would need to emulate 30-year-old designs. Merely by using readily accessible guidance systems and engines, several Third World countries should be able to develop systems with similar capabilities, only smaller, more accurate, and more reliable. Commercially available inertial navigation systems, coupled with the Global Positioning System, for instance, could provide guidance systems with better accuracy than was possible in the 1960s, given that commercial aircraft now rely on autopilots more capable than the flight controls used on cruise missiles 30 years ago.

Moreover, it should be easier to produce a strategic cruise missile like the Regulus II than a ballistic missile with a comparable range. In addition, because it is simpler to adapt cruise missiles for launch from ships and aircraft, the effective strategic range of a Third World cruise missile could be extended significantly by relying on aircraft, ships, and possibly even converted freighters as launch platforms.

Export Controls: The Missile
Technology Control Regime

In 1987, 7 countries—Canada, France, Germany, Great Britain, Italy, Japan, and the United States—formulated the Missile Technology Control Regime, a voluntary agreement to prevent the proliferation of missiles capable of delivering nuclear warheads.[6] By 1991, the MTCR had expanded to include 18 countries: the original 7 plus Australia, Austria, the 3 Benelux nations (Belgium, Luxembourg, and the Netherlands), Denmark, Finland, New Zealand, Norway, Spain, and Sweden. In addition, a number of other nations, including the former Soviet Union, had agreed to abide by its provisions, even though they did not become members.[7]

Although sometimes associated with attempts to halt the proliferation of ballistic missiles, the MTCR also covers cruise missiles and related technologies. Specifically, the agreement prohibits the export of "unmanned aerial vehicle systems (including cruise missile systems, target drones, and reconnaissance drones) capable of delivering at least a 500-kg payload to a range of 300 km." Because missiles can trade off range for payload, this prohibition extends to any missile capable of exceeding the 500-kilogram and 300-kilometer thresholds, even if the actual payload or range is lower. For example, a missile with a range of 400 kilometers and a 400-kilogram warhead would be banned if it could be modified to deliver a 500-kilogram warhead at 300 kilometers.[8]

The MTCR also limits the export of complete subsystems, components, and certain technologies considered critical to the production of cruise missiles. Such items may be exported only for use in systems that cannot achieve a range of 300 kilometers with a 500-kilogram payload. Finally, the regime prohibits the export of production facilities suitable for the manufacture of the types of missiles covered.

The success of any technology export control regime depends on its effective implementation. In the late 1970s, for example, the United States refused to sell antiship cruise missiles to a particular country (not identified publicly – perhaps Taiwan). According to an official of the Bush administration, it was discovered in 1981 that "attempts were being made [by the unidentified country] to purchase U.S.-origin missile components on a part-by-part basis."[9] In other words, the country decided that even if it could not buy a complete system, it still could acquire the missile by purchasing the individual subsystems needed to assemble it. This episode emphasizes that export controls can prevent missile proliferation only if close attention is given to the range of technologies and components that can be exploited by a creative engineer seeking to make a missile. In essence, it is much easier to prevent exports of complete missiles than it is to stop transfers of technology needed to design and manufacture a missile.

To constrain transfers of technology and components, the MTCR contains an Equipment and Technology Annex listing restricted items. The list is divided into Category I and Category II. The most sensitive items are in the first category, which includes complete missile systems and production facilities intended to make those missiles. Category II covers certain subsystems needed to make a missile. For example, item 3 in the annex, which falls into Category II, specifically forbids the export of

> (a) lightweight turbojets and turbofan engines (including turbocompound engines that are small and fuel efficient);
> (b) Ramjet/Scramjet engines. . . .

According to the annex, such engines can be exported only as an integral part of a complete manned aircraft or as a replacement part.

Obviously, the experts drafting these lists had to deal with some difficult technical problems. For example, guidance systems capable of providing a CEP of less than 10 kilometers cannot be sold unless for installation in a manned aircraft or a missile with a range of less than 300 kilometers. Yet cruise missiles can use guidance systems designed for manned aircraft, and commercially available guidance systems are capable of accuracies superior to those specified in the regime. Similarly, guidance systems for a variety of military systems are considerably more accurate than the 10-kilometer threshold. For these reasons, it appears that the language of the regime was intended to permit continued exports of guidance systems for legitimate civilian applications, as well as for military systems not prohibited by the MTCR. Implementation of the MTCR thus has required a careful examination of exports to ensure that a declared end use is not merely a cover for an activity prohibited by the regime.

Effectiveness of the MTCR

At present, the MTCR is the primary policy instrument to prevent Third World countries from acquiring cruise missiles. Because it prohibits the transfer of any cruise missiles that violate the 300-kilometer and 500-kilogram thresholds, the United States cannot export its Tomahawk and ALCM cruise missiles or France its new Apache. Even unarmed systems, such as reconnaissance drones, are covered by this ban if they exceed the MTCR limits. The MTCR thus provides an important barrier against the proliferation of long-range cruise missiles. Many countries capable of producing cruise missiles, or possessing technology to make them, now belong to the MTCR. This will significantly complicate the efforts of other nations to develop cruise missile systems.

Unfortunately, the MTCR cannot stop the spread of cruise missiles; it can only slow the speed of their proliferation. Some of the problems with the regime are inherent in any effort to prevent proliferation through export controls. Other difficulties are unique to the MTCR.

Technology Transfer. A considerable number of Third World countries can evade the technology transfer restrictions imposed by the MTCR. The technology required to make cruise missiles is similar in many respects to that needed for manned and unmanned aerial vehicles. Technology acquired for legitimate defense projects can be adapted to the requirements of cruise missiles. Thus, a country might acquire technology to make guidance systems and flight control systems for reconnaissance drones but could transfer those capabilities to cruise missile programs. Similarly, expertise with composite materials, possibly for use in fighter aircraft, might be employed to make cruise missile fuselages.

Many of the technologies needed to manufacture a cruise missile are comparable to those needed for reconnaissance drones. This is true of the Teledyne Ryan Model 324 Scarab, a remotely piloted vehicle exported by the United States to Egypt. It has an extremely accurate navigation system, relying on an inertial package that receives updates from a GPS receiver. The engine is a modified version of the turbojet used on the Harpoon antiship cruise missile. The Scarab has a range of 3,145 kilometers, but only with a 114-kilogram payload, and thus cannot carry a 500-kilogram payload.[10] Although it is unlikely that the Egyptians will convert the Scarab into a cruise missile, the RPV contains many of the basic technologies needed for such a weapon. Thus, the technology used in the Scarab could provide the basis for a cruise missile of different design.

If they cannot acquire needed technologies through legal transfers, many Third World countries have become proficient in procuring them illegally. A considerable number of proliferating countries have obtained missile components in violation of national export regulations. Among the countries alleged to have broken U.S. laws to acquire missile-related technology are Egypt, Iran, Iraq, Israel, North Korea, and South Africa.

Third World countries also can work together to evade export controls. By establishing joint rocket and missile programs, and by sharing technology and production capabilities, these nations might be able to develop systems without importing technology from countries belonging to the MTCR. North Korea has cooperated with Egypt and Iran; Iraq has worked with Argentina, Brazil, and Egypt; and Israel has shared technology over the years with Argentina, Iran, South Africa, and Taiwan.

Enforcement. The MTCR's range and payload thresholds may be difficult to enforce. The technology needed to produce a cruise missile capable of reaching 1,000 kilometers is not inherently different from that required to produce a system with a range of only 150 kilometers. The range of a cruise missile can be extended considerable distances simply by reducing the size and weight of the warhead and adding additional fuel. For example, the French Apache tactical cruise missile normally has a range of only 150 kilometers, but France is developing a version of the missile with an 800-kilometer range. The extended-range Apache is externally identical to the original missile; both versions use the same turbojet engine and guidance package. The only changes involve the warhead, which is reduced from 780 kilograms to 400 kilograms, and the fuel capacity.[11] This illustrates a key advantage of cruise missiles: unlike ballistic missiles, they need not carry an oxidizer but can rely on air to provide the oxygen needed to sustain combustion.

Fortunately, the MTCR would prohibit the transfer of a missile like the Apache because the French missile can fly more than 300 kilometers while carrying a 500-kilogram payload. Unfortunately, it would not necessarily prevent the transfer of technology associated with the Apache for use in a system that was incapable of exceeding the MTCR thresholds. For example, a guidance package suitable for use in a remotely piloted vehicle like the Egyptian Scarab, or in a decoy like Israel's Delilah, could be fitted to a cruise missile that would violate the MTCR guidelines. Almost every technology associated with a cruise missile could be reconfigured to develop a capability not prohibited by the MTCR.

Moreover, cruise missiles can be launched from aircraft with relatively little difficulty. This makes it possible to extend the effective range of a cruise missile far beyond the actual range of the weapon. The U.S. ALCM cruise missile may have a range of 2,500 kilometers, but the bomber launching it can be based 10,000 kilometers from the launch site. Even though the ASMP strategic cruise missile has a maximum range of only 250 kilometers, the French military believes that it has a strategic role because the missile is launched from long-range aircraft with a radius of up to 4,000 kilometers. In other words, the effective range of the missile is that of both the weapon and the aircraft carrying it.

In effect, air-launched cruise missiles enhance the capabilities of both the launching aircraft and the missile. An aircraft can follow a flight path that minimizes the chance of interception. Then the missile can be released at a distance from the target, where air defenses are weak, ensuring that the aircraft will survive to return to base.[12]

In conclusion, the MTCR can slow but not stop cruise missile proliferation. Unlike ballistic missiles, long-range cruise missiles share characteristics with a large number of permitted systems. In many cases, aircraft, RPV, and short-range cruise missile technology, which the MTCR does not restrict, could be of direct benefit to long-range cruise missile programs.

Arms Control

Arms control agreements could be used to constrain missile proliferation. The United States and the former Soviet

Union have had a long history of negotiating arms control treaties that focus on surface-to-surface and air-to-surface missiles. Indeed, for more than two decades the main thrust of East-West arms control has been to reach agreement on treaties that would limit such weapons. It is perhaps natural that many arms control experts believe that similar efforts involving Third World countries are necessary. Although ballistic missiles have received the lion's share of attention, most of the proposals take into account cruise missiles as well.

The U.S. Arms Control Initiative
in the Middle East

In May 1991, the Bush administration announced that it was spearheading talks to control arms in the Middle East. The initiative included specific proposals related to chemical, biological, and nuclear weapons, as well as conventional armaments and surface-to-surface missiles. A fact sheet released by the White House provides the following details regarding surface-to-surface missiles:

> The initiative proposes a freeze on the acquisition, production, and testing of surface-to-surface missiles by states in the region with a view to the ultimate elimination of such weapons from their arsenals.
> — Suppliers would also step up efforts to coordinate export licensing for equipment, technology and services that could be used to manufacture surface-to-surface missiles. Export licenses would be provided only for peaceful end uses.[13]

Exactly which missiles the proposal is intended to eliminate remains ambiguous. Clearly, ground-launched land attack cruise missiles are covered, but air-launched cruise missiles are not. Moreover, it is not evident whether the initiative applies to weapons launched from ships or submerged submarines, or whether it is intended to restrict antiship weapons. A literal reading might suggest that the proposed plan would prohibit all ASCMs except those launched from aircraft.

The general outline of the Bush administration's proposal has found considerable international acceptance. In October 1990, a report to the secretary general of the United Nations called for a freeze on the import or manufacture of long-range missiles by countries in the Middle East. Subsequently, U.S. advocates of arms control have demanded a ban on surface-to-surface missiles in the region.[14]

The Bush administration's proposal also has received some international support. In July 1991, representatives of the five permanent members of the United Nations Security Council (the P-5 countries) met in Paris to discuss regional arms control. The joint communiqué released after the meeting indicated that the five countries supported "a comprehensive program of arms control" for the Middle East. This included "a freeze and ultimate elimination of ground to ground missiles in the region." The types of missiles covered by the proposal were not specified.[15]

Global-Regional INF Agreements

Several arms control experts have suggested that the Intermediate-Range Nuclear Forces Treaty between the United States and the former Soviet Union should be extended — either globally or to specific regions of the world.[16] This would result in an agreement by Third World countries to ban all INF-capable surface-to-surface missiles.

The INF Treaty was the first arms control agreement ratified by the two superpowers to incorporate provisions constraining the deployment of cruise missiles. The treaty forbids the two countries from possessing *ground-launched* surface-to-surface missiles with a range of between 500 and 5,500 kilometers. This includes two cruise missiles: the U.S. Gryphon GLCM and the Soviet RK-55 (SSC-X-4). The INF agreement does not apply to missiles launched from aircraft, ships, or submarines; nor does it restrict missiles with ranges of less than 500 kilometers or more than 5,500 kilometers. It does cover conventionally armed missiles, however, including long-endurance harassment drones capable of flying 500 kilometers or more.

The range of a missile covered by the treaty is determined by actual performance, not by theoretical capability. The treaty indicates that the range of a missile "shall be considered . . . to be the maximum distance which can be covered by the missile in its standard design mode flying until fuel exhaustion, determined by projecting its flight path onto the earth's sphere from the launch point to the point of impact."[17] Hence, the treaty does not ban missiles whose range could be extended beyond the INF threshold unless the adaptations are part of the missile's "standard design mode."

Advocates of an extended INF Treaty argue that it is the only existing arms control agreement that bans a whole category of surface-to-surface weapons. If applied to the Middle East, such a treaty would eliminate some of the more destabilizing missiles — that is, those capable of reaching long ranges. A global or regional INF would not be a discriminatory treaty, such as the nuclear Non-Proliferation Treaty, which allows the existing nuclear powers to retain nuclear weapons while prohibiting other states from acquiring them. In contrast, Third World countries belonging to an extended INF Treaty would be treated exactly the same as the United States and Russia. Moreover, experience with the INF Treaty would facilitate its implementation in other parts of the world.

The Limitations of Arms Control

It is too early to tell whether it will be possible to negotiate arms control agreements limiting cruise missile inventories. Conceptual difficulties need to be resolved and political obstacles overcome before any meaningful progress can be made. Surface-to-surface missiles have become an increasingly important component of modern military forces. For example, virtually all countries, even those with small armies and navies, rely on defensive antitank and antiship missiles. The picture is further complicated by the extent to which some surface-to-air missiles have secondary ground attack roles. As a result, considerable care must be given to defining what categories of weapons should be included in any ban on surface-to-surface missiles in order to prevent the prohibition of weapons that military forces now consider essential for tactical operations. In addition, it is essential that a ban take into account all troubling types of weapons. A ban on surface-to-surface missiles, for example, would do nothing about air-launched cruise missiles, although they pose the same potential threat as ground-launched weapons.

The political obstacles to arms control are even more daunting than the technical ones. There is little reason to believe that it will be easy to negotiate agreements that eliminate or freeze Third World inventories of surface-to-surface missiles. The extreme difficulty in negotiating agreements between the United States and the former Soviet Union suggests that it might be even harder to reach agreement among the many states that would be involved in the proposed Middle East or global missile control agreements. The problem is especially acute in the Middle East, where many nations do not have diplomatic relations with one another and where many countries believe that resort to military force is a legitimate means of resolving political disputes.

Even if it is possible to overcome the purely diplomatic obstacles, political-military problems will have to be resolved. Third World countries have shown no inclination to accept limitations on their right to possess long-range missiles. Many believe that ballistic missiles are essential to their military forces and are certain to view with considerable skepticism any proposal that would eliminate such weapons. Similarly, countries with cruise missiles might be reluctant to give them up.

Arms control agreements could be a useful tool, but

much conceptual work still needs to be done. Although the Bush administration's proposals provide a useful starting point, many aspects of the initiative must be clarified before negotiations can proceed.

Defending against Cruise Missiles

The first defenses against cruise missiles were developed during World War II, when British air defenses worked to counter attacks by German V-1 missiles. Ultimately, Great Britain was able to protect against the V-1. This experience has only limited applicability to the challenge posed by modern land attack cruise missiles, however. Detecting and intercepting small, low-altitude cruise missiles is a difficult task, and no country appears to have developed a comprehensive solution to the problem. As a result, neither the United States nor its allies currently possess an effective counter to strikes by land attack cruise missiles.

Defending against the V-1

During World War II, the British deployed a large integrated air defense system to intercept and destroy German V-1 cruise missiles.[18] The components of this system were drawn from the highly successful air defense network that the country had created to protect against manned aircraft. It consisted of early warning and fire control radars, antiaircraft guns, barrage balloons, and fighters. The entire system was linked by a command and control system. Despite initial difficulties, eventually the British were able to shoot down virtually all V-1s fired at Allied cities.

The V-1 was the first successful cruise missile. After becoming operational in June 1944, it was employed extensively against Allied targets in England and on the Continent. By the end of the war, between 18,000 and 19,500 V-1 missiles had been fired. The missiles are believed to have killed nearly 11,000 people; another 28,000 were injured.

Allied losses would have been much higher but for an intensive bombing campaign prior to the start of the attacks that required 25,000 attack sorties to drop 36,300 tons of bombs.

The V-1 was a relatively simple weapon. It consisted of a pulse jet engine mounted on a torpedo-shaped fuselage equipped with short, stubby wings.[19] The V-1 weighed just under 2,200 kilograms and was armed with an 830-kilogram warhead. Its average range was about 240 kilometers, although some missiles traveled as far as 280 kilometers. An extended range version, capable of flying 350 kilometers, was put into service in March 1945. The V-1 attained a maximum speed of 650 kilometers per hour and cruised at an altitude of between 2,100 and 2,500 feet.

As a weapon, the V-1 had some serious defects. The ground-launched versions of the missile needed a long ramp, which meant that they had to be fired from static launchers. As a result, the V-1 system was not mobile. (Ironically, the larger and more complex V-2 ballistic missile was equipped with a mobile launcher.) Accuracy also was poor, reflecting the simplicity of the guidance system. During August 1944, the missiles demonstrated a CEP of no better than 11.4 miles. The air-launched missiles were even less accurate, with a CEP of 24 miles. Reliability was inadequate as well. Nearly 20 percent of the missiles fired at Great Britain crashed soon after launch.[20]

The characteristics of the V-1 made it vulnerable to air defenses. It could not maneuver and had to be launched in the direction of the target. This meant that the Allies could predict from which direction the V-1 missiles were likely to come and thus concentrated antiaircraft defenses in the relatively small area through which the missiles had to fly. The V-1 flew sufficiently low to make it vulnerable to antiaircraft artillery and fighters, but not low enough to avoid radar coverage. As a result, Allied air defenses were able to shoot down more than half of the V-1s that reached Great Britain. On one night late in the campaign against Great Britain, the air defenses destroyed 90 out of 97 missiles detected.

The British experience had a considerable impact on perceptions regarding the cruise missile in the postwar period. Unlike ballistic missiles, for which no defenses were devised, it was possible to defend against cruise missiles. This knowledge led many to minimize the danger they posed.

Modern Defenses

The success of the defenses against the V-1 provides little basis for estimating the capabilities of existing defenses. Modern cruise missiles like the U.S. ALCM and SLCM systems are smaller than the V-1 and fly at significantly lower altitudes. These differences are so great that many air defense experts seem to agree that it is difficult to defend against modern cruise missiles like the ALCM and Tomahawk.[21] Not only are the missiles hard to detect, but also they can be difficult to destroy.

Antiship Missile Defenses

That it is possible to defend against modern cruise missiles is suggested by the development of antiship missile defenses (ASMD) to protect naval forces. All modern navies now devote considerable resources to ASMD operations. For example, the integrated ASMD doctrine of the U.S. Navy uses area defense weapons to destroy cruise missile launch systems. At the same time, airborne early-warning aircraft and other long-range surveillance systems can provide early warning of an impending ASCM strike. Almost all U.S. Navy ships are armed with weapons capable of shooting down ASCMs—either missiles or point defense antiaircraft guns. Finally, most ships are equipped with electronic countermeasures to confuse ASCM guidance systems.

The potential effectiveness of antiship missile defenses was demonstrated during the 1973 Arab-Israeli War. The Syrian and Egyptian navies launched 54 missiles at Israeli ships, but all missed. The failure of these weapons could be attributed almost totally to ASMD. Only six years before, the Egyptians had no trouble sinking an Israeli destroyer, the Elath, with four SS-N-2 Styx antiship missiles.[22]

Since 1973, navies around the world have made an intensive effort to develop defensive systems capable of detecting and defeating antiship missiles. As a result, it is now possible for warships to defend themselves against ASCM threats. Recent experience suggests, however, that ASMD can be a difficult and expensive proposition. Moreover, there are few guarantees of success, as demonstrated by the Exocet antiship missile strikes against the Royal Navy off the Falkland Islands in 1982. The Iraqi Exocet attack on the *Stark*, a U.S. Navy frigate operating in the Persian Gulf during 1987, further emphasizes the fragility of antiship missile defenses.

Land-Based Defenses

It is more difficult to defend against land attack cruise missiles than against ASCMs. Although it is difficult to detect sea-skimming ASCMs, it is even harder to discover low-flying cruise missiles over land. Moreover, the defense against land attack cruise missiles is more complex. Because ASCMs are aimed at ships, it is possible to put the defenses exactly where the danger is the greatest. In contrast, land attack cruise missiles can aim at the whole military and civilian infrastructure of a country, so the target set is less well defined. Although defenses can be concentrated around key installations, the greater size of the locations that might be attacked creates additional problems.

Because ground-based radars can cover only a limited area when attempting to detect low-flying cruise missiles, it is necessary to rely on airborne early-warning aircraft, tower-mounted radars, or balloon-mounted radars. It may be possible to develop satellite-based radars or infrared sensors capable of detecting cruise missiles, but only the United States has the resources and the technology to deploy such systems. Regardless of the equipment used, it will be expensive for other countries to create early-warning systems. Further, the effectiveness of the systems will be open to question.

Even if it is possible to detect cruise missiles, it may be difficult to destroy them. According to one Soviet assessment, most surface-to-air missiles cannot reliably intercept and destroy modern cruise missiles.[23] SAM fire control systems may have difficulty tracking cruise missiles, especially when efforts have been made to reduce radar and infrared signatures. The warheads on SAMs have been optimized to destroy manned aircraft and may be ineffective when used against smaller cruise missiles. As a result, the SAMs may have a low probability of hitting and destroying a cruise missile target. Finally, SAM units will have only brief periods in which to engage low-flying cruise missiles. Many existing SAMs do not have the quick-reaction times needed to strike them.

Most SAM systems are optimized to engage manned aircraft flying at medium to high altitudes; few are capable of engaging targets flying at altitudes of less than 60 meters. For example, the most capable version of the ubiquitous Soviet SA-2 missile has a minimum engagement altitude of 90 meters. Even the highly capable SA-6 missile has a minimum altitude of 50 meters, although its effectiveness at such low altitudes is suspect.[24] Thus, although some SAMs are theoretically able to engage low-altitude targets, they may have difficulty shooting down cruise missiles in real-world operations.

One of the few medium-range SAMs believed capable of intercepting low-flying cruise missiles is the Soviet SA-10 Grumble. This system now comprises about 25 percent of all SAM batteries used for strategic defense by the former Soviet Union. The SA-10 missile incorporates an active radar seeker similar to the U.S. AMRAAM air-to-air missile. In addition, an SA-10 battery is equipped with the tower-mounted Flap Lid A engagement radar to facilitate attacks on low-flying targets. Although most sources credit the SA-10 with an ability to shoot down cruise missiles, it is reported to have a minimum engagement altitude of 300 meters.

This is considerably higher than the maximum altitude flown by most modern cruise missiles. The former Soviet Union has exported the SA-10 to Bulgaria, suggesting that it may be willing to sell it to other countries as well.[25]

Several Western SAM systems, such as the U.S. Army's Patriot surface-to-air missile system, should be able to shoot down low-altitude cruise missiles. In addition, many short-range SAMs, like the Franco-German Roland, should be able to destroy them. Such weapons are designed to engage low-flying targets at relatively short ranges. For this reason, short-range SAM systems can react quickly when a target appears. It is unclear, however, whether many short-range SAMs are capable of detecting and tracking cruise missiles that incorporate low-observable technologies to reduce infrared and radar signatures.

It might be possible to protect high-value targets by concentrating small antiaircraft guns in a barrier defense. Cruise missiles have relatively predictable flight paths and do not react to the presence of antiaircraft fire. As a result, they may be more vulnerable than manned aircraft to large numbers of small antiaircraft guns. Although creating extensive antiaircraft artillery defenses can be expensive, the weapons are readily available and not technologically complex.

Mine barriers are another possible solution to the cruise missile threat. Land mines capable of shooting down low-flying helicopters are now under development, and it might be possible to design these systems with a capability to destroy cruise missiles flying at low altitudes. If land mines were deployed in dense fields around high-priority targets, or along suspected cruise missile flight routes, a relatively automatic defense would be effective.

As an alternative to destruction, cruise missiles might be disrupted. Guidance systems relying on external inputs can be jammed. The ALCM and Tomahawk cruise missiles rely on a radar altimeter for the TERCOM guidance system. Hence, if a defense mechanism could disrupt the altimeter electronically, the missile would not be able to update its position. Similarly, it might be possible to disrupt satellite navigation signals.

The main problem, however, is not merely technological. Enormous resources will be needed to procure an extensive array of essential command and control systems, early-warning sensors, air defense weapons, and electronic warfare devices to defend against cruise missiles. Few Third World countries have the resources to produce or deploy such systems. Any country capable of developing a comprehensive defense against cruise missiles will almost certainly be able to deploy highly effective defenses against manned aircraft and ballistic missiles as well. But even the United States may find that the cost is too great.

In the final analysis, there is reason to believe that it will be difficult to defend against modern cruise missiles. Many of the defenses described here remain conceptual, and few of the defense systems already deployed are available to Third World countries.

Conclusion

The available evidence suggests that the proliferation of cruise missiles will become a serious problem during the 1990s. A large number of Third World countries currently possess antiship cruise missiles, and at least some probably have land attack cruise missiles as well. There is strong reason to believe that more of these nations will acquire land attack cruise missiles by the end of the decade. Moreover, it may be possible for Third World countries to produce cruise missiles with accuracies of less than 10 meters.

It is unclear whether the United States has the capability to prevent the proliferation of cruise missiles. The Missile Technology Control Regime will impede but not stop the spread of land attack cruise missiles, especially long-range systems, because it is probably impossible to prevent proliferating countries from acquiring such weapons. Arms control is only beginning to receive serious attention as a solution to the problem. Thus, it is too early to tell what obstacles will have to be overcome in the pursuit of Third World arms control agreements relating to surface-to-surface missiles. Finally, the potential effectiveness of defenses against cruise missiles is uncertain, although the technology needed to shoot down cruise missiles does exist.

Appendix A

Cruise Missile Systems of the United States, Great Britain, France, and Germany

This appendix provides summary descriptions of many of the West's better-known cruise missile systems. Not intended to be comprehensive, it rather provides a baseline for evaluating global trends in cruise missile development.

U.S. Cruise Missiles

The U.S. military is known to have at least six different cruise missile programs, although it is possible that other, classified projects also exist. Three of the programs include missiles that are armed with nuclear weapons and form a part of the strategic arsenal. Four of the programs include conventionally armed weapons. Programs have also been launched to develop harassment drones, but none is known to have entered service.

Tomahawk

There are four versions of the Tomahawk: TLAM-N, a nuclear-armed land attack missile; TASM, a conventionally armed antiship missile; TLAM-C, a conventionally armed land attack missile; and TLAM-D, a land attack missile armed with cluster munitions. A ground-launched version of the Tomahawk operated by the U.S. Air Force, known as the Gryphon or GLCM, was removed from service as a result of the INF Treaty. Each version of the missile carries different payloads and has a different guidance package.

The three TLAM versions rely on terrain comparison guidance. According to one estimate, TERCOM provides an accuracy of between 30 and 185 meters. This level of accuracy is all that is needed for nuclear-armed TLAM-N missiles but is insufficient for a conventionally armed missile. Consequently, the TLAM-C and TLAM-D also have a Digital Scene Matching Area Correlator system for terminal guidance. DSMAC compares digitized images from the planned target area with prestored scenes. The system uses a digital camera to generate images and attempts to match the scenes using a specialized imaging coprocessor capable of comparing 1 billion pixel pairs per second. Reportedly, the TLAM-C and TLAM-D have a CEP of no more than 6 meters.[1]

The antiship TASM relies on an inertial navigation system for midcourse guidance and uses a modified version of the Harpoon active radar homing seeker for terminal guidance. It carries a 450-kilogram, high-explosive warhead and has a maximum range of about 480 kilometers.

The nuclear-armed TLAM has a range of about 2,500 kilometers. In contrast, the heavier warheads of the conventionally armed TLAM-C and TLAM-D give them a maximum range of only 1,250 kilometers. Range also depends to some extent on the launch platform. When a TLAM is fired from a submarine, it is necessary to reduce the weight of the missile by eliminating some of the fuel. This means that a TLAM-C can fly only 900 kilometers when fired from a submarine. It is possible to fire a fully fueled TLAM-C from a submarine, but only by launching the missile close to the surface, which makes the submarine more vulnerable to detection. It appears that the Tomahawk missiles fired from submarines during the 1991 Persian Gulf War were fitted with full-range missiles, a minor risk given the absence of any antisubmarine threat.[2]

The TLAM-C and the TASM carry a 450-kilogram, high-explosive warhead. The TLAM-D carries 166 BLU-97/B combined effects munitions, submunitions designed for use against both personnel and light-armored vehicles. The TLAM-D can attack multiple targets. During one test of the system, a TLAM-D made cluster munition attacks on three different targets and then dived into a fourth.[3]

In 1991, the U.S. Navy was completing development of Block III improvements to the TLAM-C. A new 320-kilogram warhead was developed to replace the 450-kilogram Bullpup warhead previously used. The new warhead was as destructive as the old one, despite the reduced weight. By reducing the size and weight of the payload, it was possible to increase the amount of fuel carried. At the same time, an upgraded version of the turbofan engine was incorporated. The new Williams International W-402 engine will provide 19 percent more thrust and yet consume 2 percent less fuel. These modifications will extend the range of the missile to 1,650 kilometers, an improvement of about 30 percent. In addition, a more powerful booster motor will make it possible to fire fully fueled TLAMs from submarines at normal launch depths.[4]

Significant improvements also have been made to the guidance system. A GPS package was added to the missile, and the TLAM can now rely on either TERCOM or the Global Positioning System or both. This means that it will be possible to fire cruise missiles even when no digital maps are available, significantly enhancing the operational flexibility of the missile. It has been reported that a new version of the scene matching system, DSMAC-IIA, also will be added. According to press reports, the new terminal guidance system will be capable of storing more scenes in its memory and will be less affected by changes in scenery caused by the passing of the seasons. Finally, a time-on-target function will automatically regulate the speed of the missile to ensure that it reaches a target at a set time. This feature is critical if TLAMs are to be used in coordination with other systems, such as manned aircraft. Some of the enhancements will be made possible by incorporation of a new version of the guidance computer, which is six times more powerful than the original.[5]

Air-Launched Cruise Missile

The AGM-86B ALCM was the first successful air-launched strategic cruise missile developed by the United States. The missile entered service in 1981. The guidance system for the ALCM is almost identical to the one for the Tomahawk TLAM-N version, using a TERCOM and a high-quality inertial navigation package. Although it does not rely on a terminal guidance system, one source estimates that it has a CEP of no more than 30 meters.[6] The ALCM, like the Tomahawk, has an F-107 turbofan engine.

The production version of the ALCM has a range of about 2,400 kilometers and carries a 200-kiloton W80-1 nuclear warhead. The missile is launched from B-52 and B-1B bombers. Only about 1,700 ALCMs were ordered. The size of the program was reduced in order to fund the AGM-129A Advanced Cruise Missile.

Advanced Cruise Missile

The AGM-129A ACM, a stealthy, air-launched cruise missile, was developed to replace the AGM-86 ALCM. It is believed to have both a smaller radar cross section and a smaller infrared signature than the AGM-86. Because it can fly at lower altitudes than the ALCM, the ACM should be harder for air defenses to detect. This missile will carry the same 200-kiloton warhead as the ALCM but should have a range of at least 3,000 kilometers. The extra range will allow it to fly around heavily defended areas.[7] Although the ACM program suffered from severe contractor mismanagement, it is now being integrated into U.S. bomber units. The U.S. Air Force has contracted to buy 560 missiles and is expected to order another 455.[8]

Standoff Land Attack Missile

The AGM-84E SLAM is a land attack variant of the Harpoon.[9] Developed in the late 1980s and incorporating the airframe and other components of the Harpoon, it is considered to be an interim weapon – available until the Tri-Service Standoff Attack Missile (TSSAM) enters service. By making extensive use of existing components, contractors completed development in record time. The program was initiated immediately after the April 1986 raid on Libya, and the first test missiles were delivered in November 1988. Although the missile was not yet officially operational, the U.S. Navy was able to employ it during the 1991 Persian Gulf War.

For midcourse guidance, the SLAM relies on a GPS-aided inertial navigation system. Terminal guidance relies on a man-in-the-loop system with an imaging infrared seeker developed for the Maverick air-to-surface missile and a video data link originally used on the Walleye II television-guided glide bomb. When the missile is only one minute from the target, the data link is activated, and the weapons operator locks the missile onto the target. The missile can be launched from either the A-6E or the F/A-18, and it can be controlled from the A-6E, the F/A-18, or the A-7E. It has a range of more than 110 kilometers, but the control aircraft must be considerably closer to establish a video link with the missile.

According to press reports, seven SLAM missiles were fired at Iraqi targets during the Persian Gulf War.[10] During the first attack, an A-6E strike aircraft launched two missiles against one of Iraq's electric generation plants. An A-7E provided the final control. One of the two missiles destroyed an outer wall at the facility, and when the second missile arrived two minutes later, it was sent through the hole to destroy the generator inside the building.

Reliance on off-the-shelf solutions led to compromises in development of the system.[11] Because of a need to incorporate additional guidance systems, the airframe is 25.5 inches longer than the Harpoon, making it necessary to fly the missile with its front pointed upward. This increases drag and reduces the missile's range. A considerable amount of space and weight was wasted by the need to use readily available off-the-shelf components, which made it impossible to integrate separate components into smaller packages.

Tri-Service Standoff Attack Missile

In June 1991, the U.S. Department of Defense revealed that it had been working on a new, low-observable cruise missile since 1986. Air-launched AGM-137 and ground-launched MGM-137 versions of the Tri-Service Standoff Attack Missile are under development. The services plan to spend $15.1 billion to develop and acquire a total of 8,650 missiles. It is expected that it will cost less than $1 million to manufacture each of the missiles, although development costs drive up the total price per missile to more than $1.7 million apiece. The anticipated success of the TSSAM led the Department of Defense to cancel U.S. participation in the multinational MSOW program.[12]

Few characteristics of the TSSAM have been released. According to the Pentagon, it will weigh 1,040 kilograms and will have a range greater than 185 kilometers. The maximum range of the ground-launched version will be under the 500-kilometer limit set by the INF Treaty, and the air-launched version will have a range of less than 600 kilometers. For reduced vulnerability to hostile air defenses, the missile incorporates low-observable technologies. One analyst has estimated that the TSSAM could carry a warhead of 450 kilograms.[13] The U.S. Air Force will mount the AGM-137 on B-2 and B-52 bombers and F-16 fighters, the U.S. Navy intends to equip F/A-18 fighters and A-6 attack aircraft with the same version, and the U.S. Army will launch MGM-137 missiles from MLRS launchers.

The MGM-137 will be armed with a new submunition, known as the Brilliant Anti-Tank weapon. Designed for use primarily against tanks, the BAT is reported to be one of the most sophisticated submunitions ever developed. According to press reports, the system will employ a combination of acoustic and infrared sensors to acquire targets. The U.S. Army plans to spend $344 million developing the BAT, but the overall cost of the program is expected to reach $2.2 billion by the end of production.[14]

Have Slick

The Have Slick designation refers to a once-classified air-to-surface missile development program about which little is known. According to one source, McDonnell Douglas is producing the missile for use with new-generation fighter aircraft. Another report claims that the missile will have a range of 500 kilometers and that it will carry a 700-kilogram payload consisting of submunitions or small missiles. Have Slick was scheduled to begin flight tests in 1990 or 1991, and development was to end in 1993.[15] The limited information available makes it impossible to determine the differences between Have Slick and TSSAM.

Long-Range Conventional Standoff Weapon (LRCSW)

The LRCSW was a design program established in 1989 to develop a conventionally armed cruise missile with a range of over 3,000 kilometers. The original plans called for the missile to enter service in 2001. The long range of the missile was an anticipated benefit of a new generation of propfan engines, which use turbines to drive propellers. It was expected to have near-zero CEP accuracy. The U.S. Air Force and the U.S. Navy planned to buy between 2,500 and 10,000 LRCSWs at a cost of $750,000 to $1.5 million each.[16] The program never got out of the exploratory phase, however, because the propfan engines proved incapable of producing the expected range.[17]

Harassment Drones

The United States has long contemplated acquiring small, ground-launched antiradiation missiles. In the early 1980s, the U.S. Air Force developed the Pave Tiger, but the system ran into difficulties and was canceled. Currently, consideration is being given to procurement of another system under the Seek Spinner program. Two systems are being explored: the Brave, a descendant of the Pave Tiger produced by Boeing, and the Harpy II, developed by Israel Aircraft Industries.[18] The U.S. Air Force also funded development of the AGM-136A Tacit Rainbow, an air-launched, turbojet-powered missile that flies to a predesignated target area, where it loiters while searching for targets.[19] After encountering problems, however, the program was terminated before any missiles were placed in the inventory.

British Cruise Missiles

At present, the British military operates a number of foreign-built cruise missiles, including the U.S. sub-launched Harpoon and the French Exocet ASCMs. It has one domestically produced missile, the Sea Eagle ASCM. In addition, the Royal Air Force is contemplating acquisition of a long-range, nuclear-armed cruise missile. Among the alternatives being considered are two U.S. systems, the SRAM-T and the AQM-127A SLAT, and the French ASLP.[20]

The Sea Eagle ASCM entered service in the mid-1980s.[21] The Sea Eagle has a conventional guidance arrangement, using an inertial navigation system for midcourse guidance and an active homing radar for terminal guidance. Powered by a French Micro-turbo TRI-60-1 turbojet engine, the 600-kilogram missile has a range of more than 110 kilometers and carries a 230-kilogram warhead. It has been exported to India.

French Cruise Missiles

Cruise missiles have become an increasingly important component of the French arsenal. Currently, France has one strategic cruise missile in its inventory, the ASMP, which it plans to replace with a new missile, the ASLP, in the 1990s. In addition, a conventionally armed cruise missile, the Apache, is now under development.

ASMP

The French began development of the ASMP nuclear-armed supersonic cruise missile in 1978.[22] The first flight tests took place in 1983, and the missile entered service in 1986. A total of 100 ASMP missiles were built at a cost of about FFr 4 billion (about $500 million). This relatively small missile weighs 840 kilograms and is capable of carrying a 300-kiloton warhead.

The ASMP can be launched from Mirage IVP bombers, Mirage 2000N fighter-bombers, and carrier-based Super Etendard attack aircraft. A liquid-fuel ramjet engine gives the missile a potential speed of Mach 3.5. When fired at high altitudes, it generally flies at Mach 3 and has a maximum range of 250 kilometers. When launched at low altitudes, the maximum speed is reduced to Mach 2 and the range drops to only about 80 kilometers. The naval version of the missile is normally fired to ranges of 60 kilometers or less.

The ASMP relies on an inertial guidance system, which is updated by the launch aircraft immediately before the missile is released. This means that its accuracy depends in part on the accuracy of the initial data received from the launch aircraft. The missile is capable of flying a preprogrammed terrain-following flight path intended to go around air defenses and to exploit radar-masking terrain.

Apache

The air-launched Apache will have a range of 150 kilometers and will be capable of carrying a payload of 780 kilograms and delivering ordnance with an accuracy of about 1 meter. The missile will fly at Mach 0.9 and will have "low radar and IR signatures." It will have "very-low-level terrain-following flight capability." The total cost of the Apache program will be about FFr 10 billion ($1.59 billion), which will provide the French Air Force with 500 missiles. This includes FFr 2 billion ($320 million) for development of the airframe and the submunitions, so the unit production cost is estimated at FFr 16 million ($2.5 million). The French Air Force will begin receiving Apaches in 1996, but the missile may be available for export as early as 1994.[23]

Matra has announced that it intends to develop an extended-range version of the Apache, known as the Super-Apache. This system will reduce the weight of the warhead to only 400 kilograms. It appears that the weight saved will be used to increase the amount of fuel carried by the missile, making it possible to give the Super-Apache a range of 800 kilometers – six times that of the original missile.[24]

ASLP

In mid-1991, the French government announced that it intended to replace the ASMP with a new air-launched cruise missile, the ASLP. Like the ASMP, the ASLP will be a supersonic cruise missile, but it will have a range "several times longer." In addition, the ASLP will have "low radar detectability." Current plans call for the missile to be fired from the Rafale, a new tactical fighter currently under development in France. According to another report, the ASLP will have a range of 1,000 to 1,300 kilometers and will cruise at speeds of Mach 3 to 4.[25]

German Cruise Missiles

The German military has shown considerable interest in cruise missiles and has invested substantial resources in harassment drones for antiradiation and antitank missions. The Germans have built the Kormoran antiship missile and are collaborating with the French to build the ANS supersonic ASCM.

Kormoran

The Kormoran ASCM was produced in December 1977, following a ten-year development process.[26] The 600-kilogram missile carries a 160-kilogram warhead and has a range of more than 30 kilometers. This rocket-powered missile uses the same combination of INS midcourse guidance and active radar terminal guidance as that on most antiship missiles. The Kormoran 2 version, which entered production around 1988, has a range of more than 55 kilometers and a 220-kilogram warhead. The Kormoran is operated only by Germany and Italy.

Harassment Drones

The DAR antiradar drone has been under development since the mid-1980s. Like the Israeli Harpy, the DAR is a surface-launched, piston-powered, armed harassment drone. Using a seeker now being constructed by Texas Instruments, the DAR will look for search and fire control radars. Reportedly, the British Ministry of Defense also is interested in the system. The DAR is scheduled to be in production from 1994 to 1999.[27]

A more sophisticated concept is the West German antitank harassment drone, the KDH (Kampfdrohne des Heeres). This weapon, expected to enter service in the late 1990s, will attack tanks and self-propelled artillery in rear areas. It will operate autonomously, meaning that it will be able to detect and identify potential targets without human intervention. The Germans expect to procure several thousand drones.[28]

Appendix B

Missile Systems and Components Produced in the Third World and Elsewhere, by Country

117

TABLE B-1
Production of Remotely Piloted Vehicles in the Third World, 1990

Country	System	Description
Argentina	Quimar MQ-1 Chimango	Version of Italian Mirach 70; possible export sales to Iran, Peru, and South Africa.
	Quimar MQ-2 Bigua	Version of Mirach 100 for use as an antiradiation harassment drone.
	Quimar Agilucho	A version of Italian Mirach 20.
Brazil	Aeromot K1 AM	Adapted from Northrop KD2R-5 target drone.
	CBT BQM-1BR	Reconnaissance RPV designed in the early 1980s using an indigenously developed turbojet. There are no indications that it was ever put into production.
	CTA Acaua (Hawk)	Mini-RPV under development in the late 1980s, capable of carrying a television camera.
India	Mini-RPV	Mini-RPV claimed to have a low-radar signature. It weighs 120 kg., relies on a 26-hp engine, and can carry a 25-kg. payload.
	Large Mini-RPV	A new mini-RPV with a 38-hp engine, weighing 250 kg. with a 45-kg. payload.
	MT	Supersonic drone, allegedly developed as a target for surface-to-air missiles. Released from aircraft, it has a maximum speed of Mach 1.4 and a range of 35 to 70 km.
	ADE PTA	Ostensibly a target drone. PTA is a 400-kg. drone launched using a rocket booster. It has a turbojet engine with a thrust of 400 kg. Capable of speeds of up to Mach 0.8, it has a maximum endurance of about 1 hour.

Indonesia	LAPAN XTG-01	Experimental mini-RPV test flown in the late 1970s.
Iran	Shahin	First shown in May 1989. Radio control. Twin booms with propeller in the rear.
	Baz	First shown in May 1989. Radio control. Simple design with front-mounted prop.
	"22006"	First shown in May 1989. Radio control. Rear-mounted prop.
Iraq	Al-Yamama	First shown in May 1989 but started development in 1986. Prototype flew in 1987. A prop-driven mini-RPV similar in design to the Israeli Pioneer system.
	Marakub 100	First shown in May 1989. Iraqi version of Italian Meteor Mirach 100. Fiberglass body made in Iraq, but engines and guidance imported.
Israel	Scout	Mini-RPV developed by Israel Aircraft Industries in the late 1970s and early 1980s. Used for reconnaissance during the 1982 Lebanon War.
	Delilah	Turbojet-powered harassment drone operating as an antiradiation missile. Can be launched from the air or the ground. Carries a 50-kg. payload. Used during the 1982 Lebanon War.
	Harpy	Harassment drone for use against radar systems.
	Mastiff	Mini-RPV developed by Tadiran in the late 1970s and early 1980s. Fitted with a TV camera and used for reconnaissance during the 1982 Lebanon War.

(Table continues.)

119

TABLE B-1 (*continued*)

Country	System	Description
	Pioneer	Mini-RPV developed by Israeli companies for the U.S. Coproduced in the U.S. by AAI Corp., the Pioneer was used extensively during the 1991 Persian Gulf War.
	Impact	New mini-RPV to replace the Pioneer.
Saudi Arabia	MCS PL-90	Mini-RPV test-flown in the early 1970s in the U.S. and sold by its U.S. developer to Saudi Arabia in 1979. It is unknown if the Saudis actually began production of the system.
South Africa	National Dynamics Eyrie 6A-60	Mini-RPV with a maximum range of 1,750 km. and an endurance of 13 hours. Uses a 60-hp engine and a pusher prop. Can be equipped with several cameras.
	Armscor Seeker	Mini-RPV with a pusher prop and a 25-hp engine. Payload of 40 kg. and a maximum speed of 65 knots. Endurance of 9 hours.
South Korea	Daewoo long-endurance RPV	Long-endurance reconnaissance RPV now under development.
	Korean Air KD2R-5	Licensed copy of this Northrop target drone.

Sources: Kenneth Munson, *World Unmanned Aircraft* (New York: Jane's, 1988); Robert Salvy and Gowri Sundaram, "Oriental Industry Comes of Age," *International Defense Review*, March 1990, p. 245; Dan Boyle and Robert Salvy, "Iranian RPVs," *International Defense Review*, June 1989, p. 857; Guy Willis, "Open Sesame! Baghdad Show Reveals Iraqi Military-Industrial Capabilities," *International Defense Review*, June 1989, p. 838; "Korean Air Negotiates Agreement to Coproduce UH-60," *Aviation Week and Space Technology*, June 12, 1989, p. 227; "Armscor: If You Can't Buy It, Make It," *Armada International*, January 1989, pp. 60–61.

TABLE B-2
Combat Aircraft Production in the Third World, 1990

Country	Aircraft	Description
Argentina	IA 58A Pucara	Turboprop training and light attack aircraft used by the Argentinian Air Force since the late 1970s.
	IA 63 Pampa	Advanced jet trainer designed with assistance from Dornier (FRG) and equipped with U.S. engines.
Brazil	AT-25 Xavante	License-built version of the Aermacchi MB-326GC (Italy).
	AMX[a]	Light strike aircraft developed in cooperation with Aermacchi (Italy).
Chile	A-36 Halcon	Version of Spanish CASA C-101CC-02 turbojet-powered light attack plane. Assembled and partially manufactured in Chile.
Egypt	Alphajet	Light strike aircraft built under license from Dassault (France).
India	MiG-21	Supersonic fighter built under license from the Soviet Union.
	MiG-27M	License-built version of a Soviet supersonic attack aircraft.
	Jaguar	Light attack aircraft built under license from Great Britain.
	LCA[a]	The Light Combat Aircraft is a supersonic fighter designed in India but uses components and technology acquired from the U.S.

(Table continues.)

TABLE B-2 (*continued*)

Country	Aircraft	Description
Iraq	Fao[c]	Jet trainer–light strike aircraft, originally known as Saad 25 program. License production of foreign aircraft. Contenders include British Aerospace Hawk, Dassault Alphajet, Aermacchi MB 339C, CASA C101, and Czech L-39. Program never finalized.
Israel	Kfir	Unauthorized copy of French Mirage 5 supersonic fighter, using U.S. J79 engine to replace original French Atar engine. Has improved avionics and better performance than original.
	Phantom 2000	Rebuilt F-4E fighters with new avionics.
	Lavi[b]	Advanced technology supersonic fighter. Canceled under pressure from the U.S. owing to high cost of development and production of aircraft.
North Korea	MiG-21	Copies of Soviet MiG-21, possibly relying on imported components.
Singapore	A4-S Skyhawk	Completely rebuilt Skyhawk attack aircraft with new avionics and F-404 engines.
South Africa	Mirage F-1	License-built version of the French aircraft.
	Impala	License-built version of the Italian Aermacchi MB-326 light attack aircraft and trainer.
	CAVA[c]	A project to develop a new-generation supersonic fighter aircraft.

122

South Korea	F-5E/F	Sixty-eight were assembled in South Korea from 1981 to 1986 using components supplied by Northrop.
	FSX[a]	Program to produce license-built version of the F-16 supersonic fighter, modified with assistance from U.S. companies.
Taiwan	F-5E/F	License production from Northrop (U.S.) of this supersonic fighter starting in 1973.
	IDF[a]	Supersonic fighter designed in Taiwan but received considerable technical assistance from the U.S. Engines and avionics are modified versions of U.S. systems.

Sources: John W. R. Taylor, *Jane's All the World's Aircraft, 1987–88* (New York: Jane's, 1987); Michael J. H. Taylor, *NATO Major Combat Aircraft* (London: Tri-Service Press, 1989). On North Korean production of MiG-21s, see "Official Says North to Produce MiG-21 by 1995," Seoul KBS-1 Television, August 29, 1991, as cited in FBIS-EAS-91-169, August 30, 1991, p. 29, and "Air Force Day Commemoration Announced," Naewoe Tongsin, No. 655, September 1, 1989, pp. 1J–4J, as cited in FBIS-EAS-89-220, November 16, 1989, pp. 15–16.

[a]Systems under development.
[b]Systems never built.
[c]Systems planned.

TABLE B-3
Engines Produced for Cruise Missiles

Country	Company	Model	Thrust (lb)	Weight (lb)	Applications
China	?	Wopen	?	?	C802
France	Societe Turbomeca	Arbizon 3B	907	253	OTOMAT
		Arbizon 4	741	132	Hsiung Feng II
		Arbizon 5	1,046	110	Under development
	Microturbo	TRS 18	254	81.5	Mirach 100
		TRS 18-1	337	85	Mirach 100-3
		TRI 60-1	787	108	Sea Eagle
		TRI 60-2	832	108	RBS15
		TRI 60-30	1,050	123	Under development for Apache
Great Britain	Noel Penny Turbines	NPT 151-4	105	66	Delilah
		NPT 171	170	55.5	Brave 3000
		NPT 401B	400	100	Mirach 100 ER
		NPT 901	900	165	Under development
India	Hindustan Aeronautics (HAL)	PTAE-7	1,433		PTA

Israel	Bet Shemesh	Sorek 4	809	133	Gabriel 4?
	Israel Military Industries (IMI)	?	–	–	Designation and characteristics unknown
South Africa	ARMSCOR	APA 1	740	?	Skorpioen II
United States	Teledyne CAE	J402-CA-400	660	102	Harpoon
		J402-CA-701	725	113	?
		J402-CA-702	960	135	MQM-107
		382-10	1,000	135	Under development
	Williams	F107-WR-101	600	146	ALCM
	International	F107-WR-400	600	144	SLCM/GLCM

Sources: The basic sources are Munson, *World Unmanned Aircraft;* "U.S. Gas Turbine Engines," *Aviation Week and Space Technology*, March 20, 1989, pp. 177, 179; "International Gas Turbine Engines," *Aviation Week and Space Technology*, March 20, 1989, pp. 180–181. Additional data came from "Turbojet Updates China's C 801," *Jane's Defence Weekly*, February 25, 1989, p. 321; Edwin S. Townsley and Clarence A. Robinson, "Critical Technology Assessment in Israel and NATO Nations," Institute for Defense Analyses, IDA Memorandum Report M-317, April 1987, pp. III-54; "The Armaments Corporation of South Africa at FIDA '86," *Military Technology*, July 1986, p. 115.

TABLE B-4
Cruise Missile Production Worldwide

Country	Missile	Type	Status	Range (km.)	Warhead (kg.)	Using Countries	Comments
Argentina	MQ-2 Bigua	land attack; antiship	D	900	40–70	Argentina?	Armed version of Argentinian copy of Mirach-100 reconnaissance drone.
Brazil	Barracuda	antiship	D	70	?		Rocket-powered.
China	HY-2 Silkworm	antiship	S	95	513	Bangladesh, China, Egypt, Iran, Iraq, North Korea, Pakistan	Improved version of Soviet SS-N-2 Styx.
	HY-4	antiship	S	135	500	China?	Improved HY-2.
	C 601	antiship	S	100	513	China, Iraq	Air-launched version of HY-2.
	C 201	antiship	S?	135	500	China?	HY-4 with upgraded electronics.
	HY-3/C 101/ C 301	antiship	D?	50	?		Ramjet-powered missiles under development in late 1980s, as well

	Name	Type				Comments
						as air-launched version. HY-3 may have extended range.
	C 801	antiship	S	40	165	China	An air-launched version of the C 801 missile has a 50-km. range.
	C 802	antiship	D	90	165		Turbojet-powered version of C 801.
	C 611	antiship	S	?	?	Iraq?	Extended-range version of the C 601.
France	Exocet MM40	antiship	S	65	165	Argentina, Bahrain, Belgium, Brazil, Brunei, Cameroon, Chile, Colombia, Ecuador, France, Germany, Great Britain, Greece, Indonesia,	Surface-launched version. Also submarine (SM-39) and aircraft (AM-39) versions.

(Table continues.)

127

TABLE B-4 (*continued*)

Country	Missile	Type	Status	Range (km.)	Warhead (kg.)	Using Countries	Comments
						Iraq, Kuwait, Malaysia, Morocco, Nigeria, Oman, Pakistan, Peru, Qatar, South Korea, Thailand, Tunisia, United Arab Emirates	
	ASMP	strategic	S	350	?	France	Carries 300-kiloton nuclear warhead. Maximum speed is Mach 3.5.
	ASLP	strategic	D	1,000–1,300	?		Replacement for ASMP. Maximum speed of Mach 3–4.
	ANS	antiship	D	180	180		Mach 2 replacement for the Exocet under development with Germany.

128

Country	Name	Mission				Countries	Comments
	Super-Apache	land attack	D	800	400		Extended range version of Apache. Identical to Apache except for smaller warhead.
	Apache	land attack	D	150	780		Air-launched missile with accuracy of 1 m. using radar guidance systems.
Germany	Kormoran 2	antiship	S	55+	220	Germany, Italy	Air-launched, rocket-powered.
	KDAR	harassment drone	D	80–100 (effective)	?		Antiradiation.
	KDH	harassment drone	D	?	?		Antitank.
Great Britain	Sea Eagle	antiship	S	110	230	Germany, Great Britain, India	Turbojet-powered.
Iraq	Ababil	land attack?	D?	500?	200?		Apparently a modified version of Mirach 600 RPV.

(Table continues.)

TABLE B-4 (*continued*)

Country	Missile	Type	Status	Range (km.)	Warhead (kg.)	Using Countries	Comments
	Faw 70	antiship	S?	70	500	Iraq?	Iraqi version of Soviet SS-N-2C. Also versions with ranges of 150 km. and 200 km.
Israel	Popeye (Have Nap in U.S.)	land attack	S	100		Israel, United States	Air-launched, rocket-powered missile with inertial guidance and TV terminal guidance.
	Delilah	harassment drone	S	400	54	Israel	Turbojet-powered, antiradiation decoy. Can be launched from air or ground. Used in 1982 Lebanon War.

Harpy	harassment drone	S	500+	Israel	?	Ground-launched propeller-driven antiradiation weapon.
Gabriel I/II	antiship	S	40	Chile, Ecuador, Israel, Kenya, Singapore, South Africa, Taiwan, Thailand	180	Data refer to Gabriel II, which incorporates TV-terminal guidance. Can be used against land targets.
Gabriel III	antiship	S	36	Israel	150	First version of Gabriel with active radar guidance. Air-launched version with 60 + km. range.
Gabriel IV	antiship	S?	200	Israel	150–200	Turbojet-powered.

(Table continues.)

TABLE B-4 (continued)

Country	Missile	Type	Status	Range (km.)	Warhead (kg.)	Using Countries	Comments
Italy	OTOMAT Mk. 2	antiship	S	180	210	Egypt, Italy, Kenya, Libya, Nigeria, Peru, Saudi Arabia, Venezuela	OTOMAT Mk. 1 has a range of only 80 km. Turbojet-powered, ship-launched missile.
Japan	ASM-1	antiship	S	50	250	Japan	Air-launched, rocket-powered.
	SSM-1	antiship	S	150	250	Japan	Turbojet-powered. Can be launched from land, surface ships, or submarines.
North Korea	HY-2	antiship	S	95	513	Iran, North Korea	Licensed version of Chinese HY-2 Silkworm. Previously, North Korea produced the HY-1.
Norway	Penguin Mk. 3	antiship	S	40+	120	Greece, Norway, Sweden, Turkey, United States	Infrared terminal guidance.

Country	Name	Mission				Source	Remarks
South Africa	Skorpioen II	antiship	D?	?	?	South Africa?	Turbojet-powered.
Sweden	Rb 08A	antiship	S	250	250		Modified version of French CT.20 target drone.
	RBS 15	antiship	S	70	250	Finland, Sweden, Yugoslavia?	Air-launched version has 150-km. range.
	ASOM	land attack	D	?	?		Glider weapon that may be developed in powered version. Radar guidance for meter-level accuracy.
Taiwan	Hsiung Feng I	antiship	S	40	70?	Taiwan	Copy of Israeli Gabriel II.
	Hsiung Feng II	antiship	S	180?	?	Taiwan	Turbojet-powered.
USSR (former Soviet Union)	SS-N-21 Sampson	strategic	S	3,000	?	former Soviet Union	Nuclear-armed, turbojet-powered, submarine-launched missile.

(*Table continues.*)

TABLE B-4 (*continued*)

Country	Missile	Type	Status	Range (km.)	Warhead (kg.)	Using Countries	Comments
	AS-15 Kent	strategic	S	3,000	?	former Soviet Union	Nuclear-armed, turbojet-powered, aircraft-launched missile.
	SS-NX-24	strategic	D	4,000–7,400?	?		Submarine-launched supersonic missile.
	AS-X-19	strategic	D	?	?		Air-launched missile with longer range than AS-15. Possibly a supersonic weapon.
	SS-N-22 Sunburn	antiship	S	125?	450	former Soviet Union	Ship-launched Mach 2.5 missile.
	SS-N-19 Shipwreck	strategic? antiship	S	555	?	former Soviet Union	Large supersonic missile launched from surface ships and submarines.

134

Name	Type		Range 1	Range 2	Country	Description
SS-N-12 Sandbox	antiship	S	555	1,000	former Soviet Union	Mach 2.5 missile launched from ships and sur-faced-submarines. Can carry a nucle-ar warhead.
SS-N-9 Siren	antiship	S	120	500	former Soviet Union	Ship- and subma-rine-launched.
SS-N-7 Starbright	antiship	S	65	500	former Soviet Union	Submarine-launched, rocket-powered.
SS-N-3 Shad-dock/SSC-1 Sepal	strategic; antiship	S	460	1,000	former Soviet Union, Syria, Yugoslavia	Conventionally and nuclear-armed versions. Launched from land, surface ships, and sur-faced submarines. SS-N-3C has a range of 740 km.

(Table continues.)

TABLE B-4 (*continued*)

Country	Missile	Type	Status	Range (km.)	Warhead (kg.)	Using Countries	Comments
	SS-N-2C Styx	antiship	S	83	500	Algeria, Angola, Cuba, Egypt, Ethiopia, Finland, India, Libya, North Korea, Somalia, former Soviet Union, Syria, Vietnam, Yemen, Yugoslavia	Latest version of SS-N-2 family of ship-launched missiles. SS-N-2A has an effective range of only 30 km.
	AS-5 Kelt	land attack; antiship	S	230	1,000	Egypt, Iraq, former Soviet Union	Antiradiation version for land attack.
	AS-6 Kingfish	strategic? antiship	S	560	1,000	Iraq? former Soviet Union	Mach 3.5 missile, can be used against ships or land targets. Can be nuclear-armed.
	AS-4 Kitchen	strategic; antiship;	S	460	1,000	former Soviet Union	Mach 3.5 missile that can be nucle-

Name		Type		Range		Deployed by	Notes
							ar-armed. Land attack version with antiradiation guidance system.
AS-3 Kangaroo	strategic	S	650	?		former Soviet Union	Nuclear-armed Mach 1.8 missile. Turbojet engine.
AS-2 Kipper	antiship	S	200	1,000		Soviet Union	Turbojet-powered Mach 1.2 missile.
AS-1/SS-C-2 Kennel	antiship	S	100	700–1,000		Bulgaria, Cuba, East Germany, Egypt, Poland, Romania, former Soviet Union, Syria	SS-C-2 antiship version has a range of only 25 km.
United States	Harpoon	antiship	S	220	222	Australia, Canada, Denmark, Egypt, Germany, Great Britain, Greece, Indonesia, Iran, Israel, Japan, Netherlands,	Turbojet-powered missile available in versions launched from aircraft, ships, and submarines.

(Table continues.)

TABLE B-4 (*continued*)

Country	Missile	Type	Status	Range (km.)	Warhead (kg.)	Using Countries	Comments
						Pakistan, South Korea, Saudi Arabia, Singapore, Spain, Thailand, Turkey, United States	
	SLAM	land attack	S	110+		United States	Version of Harpoon with TV-terminal guidance.
	AGM-86B ALCM	strategic	S	2,400		United States	Nuclear-armed.
	AGM-129A Advanced Cruise Missile (ACM)	strategic	S	3,000		United States	Stealthy air-launched, nuclear-armed missile.

Tomahawk TLAM-N	strategic	S	2,500		United States	Nuclear-armed.
Tomahawk TASM	antiship	S	480	480	United States	Modified Harpoon guidance package.
Tomahawk TLAM-D	land attack	S	1,250	450	United States	Carries 166 BLU-97/B combined effects munitions.
Tomahawk TLAM-C Block III	land attack	S	1,650	320	United States	Enhanced version of original TLAM-C.
Have Slick	land attack	D	?	?		New land attack missile now under development.
TSSAM	land attack	D	less than 600	450?		Air-launched version for U.S. Air Force and Navy. Ground-launched version carries BAT anti-tank submunition.

(Table continues.)

TABLE B-4 (continued)

Country	Missile	Type	Status	Range (km.)	Warhead (kg.)	Using Countries	Comments
	Tacit Rainbow	harassment drone	D	100?	18		Development ended without system entering service. Air-launched system developed, but ground-launched version also planned. Turbojet-powered with a maximum endurance of 80 minutes.

Sources: Norman Friedman, *World Naval Weapons Systems* (Annapolis: U.S. Naval Institute Press, 1989); Bill Gunston, *Illustrated Encyclopedia of Aircraft Armament* (New York: Orion Books, 1988); International Institute for Strategic Studies, *The Military Balance, 1990–1991* (London: Brassey's for the International Institute for Strategic Studies, 1990); A. D. Baker III, *Combat Fleets of the World, 1990/1991: Their Ships, Aircraft, and Armaments*, Bernard Prezelin, ed. (Annapolis: U.S. Naval Institute Press, 1990). See also sources cited in the appendix and text.

Notes

Chapter 1

1. A more complete account of the use of the TLAM and SLAM cruise missiles in the Persian Gulf War appears in chapter 2. They are described in appendix A, this volume.

2. One of the first discussions of this problem appears in James Roche, "Weapons Proliferation in the Middle East," *Between Two Administrations: An American-Israeli Dialogue* (Washington, D.C.: Washington Institute for Near East Policy, 1989), 52–53.

3. I previously examined this subject in *Ballistic Missiles in Modern Conflict*, Washington Paper no. 146 (New York: Praeger Center for Strategic and International Studies, 1991) (first published in 1990 as *Ballistic Missiles in the Third World: Threat and Response* by the same press). Two other detailed studies of Third World ballistic missile proliferation are Aaron Karp, "Ballistic Missile Proliferation in the Third World," *SIPRI Yearbook 1989* (New York: Oxford University Press for the Stockholm International Peace Research Institute, 1989), 287–318, and Robert D. Shuey et al., "Missile Proliferation: Survey of Emerging Missile Forces," Congressional Research Service (CRS), 88-642F, October 3, 1988, as revised February 9, 1989. The broad context of missile proliferation is examined in Janne Nolan, *Trappings of Power: Ballistic Missiles in the Third World* (Washington: Brookings Institution, 1991).

4. Carus, *Ballistic Missiles*, 3–11.

5. These statements are based on David F. Bond, "Intelligence Agencies See Weaker Warsaw Pact Threat," *Aviation Week and Space Technology*, January 26, 1990, p. 28. A different version of the Webster testimony appears in the *New York Times* and other sources. Apparently, many of these accounts were based on a prepared statement and do not correspond with what Judge Webster actually said. See Michael Wines, "Congress Starts Review of U.S. Military Posture," *New York Times*, January 24, 1990, p. A11.

6. In addition to the sources cited in note 2 above, I analyzed these developments in "Trends and Implications of Missile Proliferation," a paper presented at a meeting of the International Studies Association, Washington, D.C., April 13, 1990.

7. The six Third World countries to use ballistic missiles are Afghanistan (against guerrilla forces starting in late 1989), Egypt (against Israel during the 1973 Arab-Israeli War), Iran (against Iraq and Kuwait during the 1980–1988 Iran-Iraq War), Iraq (against Iran in the 1980–1988 Iran-Iraq War and against Israel and Saudi Arabia in the 1991 Persian Gulf War), Libya (against a U.S. installation on an Italian island in 1986), and Syria (against Israel during the 1973 Arab-Israeli War).

8. Eric H. Arnett, *Sea-Launched Cruise Missiles and U.S. Security* (New York: Praeger, 1991), provides a recent discussion of cruise missiles and related technologies; it was published after this study was prepared.

9. John C. Toomay, "Technical Characteristics," *Cruise Missiles: Technology, Strategy, Politics*, Richard K. Betts, ed. (Washington: Brookings Institution, 1981), 31.

10. Missiles relying on both air-breathing and rocket engines were included in a widely reproduced chart of U.S. and Soviet cruise missiles originally prepared in 1979 for Rear Admiral Walter M. Locke when he was director of the Joint Cruise Missiles Project. See Michael Armitage, *Unmanned Aircraft*, Brassey's Air Power and Weapons Systems and Technology Series, vol. 3 (Washington, D.C.: Brassey's Defence Publishers, 1988), 61. To further complicate matters, many jet-powered cruise missiles use solid-fuel booster rockets. The air-launched version of the Harpoon, for example, relies only on its turbojet engine, but the ship-launched version requires a booster rocket to launch the missiles.

11. See the discussion of ASCMs in the Statement of Rear

Admiral Thomas A. Brooks, U.S. Navy, Director of Naval Intelligence, before the U.S. House, Subcommittee on Seapower, Strategic, and Critical Materials, Armed Services Committee on Intelligence Issues, March 7, 1991, pp. 71–74.

12. For an authoritative description of the MTCR, see Richard H. Speier, "The Missile Technology Control Regime," *Chemical Weapons & Missile Proliferation—With Implications for the Asia/Pacific Region*, Trevor Findlay, ed. (Boulder, Colo.: Lynn Rienner Publishers, 1991), 115–121.

13. The resolution states:

> 8. [The Security Council] decides that Iraq unconditionally accept the destruction, removal, or rendering harmless, under international supervision, of:
>
> . . . .
>
> (b) all ballistic missiles with a range greater than 150 kilometers and related major parts, and repair and production facilities.

Chapter 2

1. U.S. Department of Defense, *Soviet Military Power, 1990* (Washington, D.C.: U.S. Government Printing Office, 1990), 53–55.

2. Bill Gunston, *The Illustrated Encyclopedia of Aircraft Armament* (New York: Orion Books, 1988), 111.

3. According to Statement of Rear Admiral Thomas A. Brooks before the U.S. House, Subcommittee on Seapower, Strategic, and Critical Materials, 72–73.

4. Melissa Healy and Ralph Vartabedian, "Secret Work by Northrop on Missile Told," *Los Angeles Times*, June 7, 1991, pp. A1, A28.

5. Carol Reed, "Matra Plans New Cruise Missile," *Jane's Defence Weekly*, June 29, 1991, p. 1168.

6. Nick Cook, "Saab Seeks ASOM Missile Partner," *Jane's Defence Weekly*, June 1, 1991, p. 912.

7. A disadvantage of ARM harassment drones like the Harpy is their slow reaction time. A supersonic Harm ARM can be launched against radars at ranges of more than 80 kilometers and will take no longer than 3 minutes to reach the target. In contrast, it would take the Harpy at least 30 minutes to cover the same

distance. The advantages of the faster Harm in this respect are obvious.

8. Brigitte Sauerwein, "Unmanned Aerial Vehicles, Part 1: European Programs – Federal Republic of Germany," *International Defense Review*, April 1989, p. 456.

9. The BAT is an antitank submunition using acoustic and infrared sensors. For a discussion of what is currently known about this weapon, see the appendix.

10. No attempt will be made here to systematically compare the relative advantages of manned aircraft, ballistic missiles, and cruise missiles. Clearly, there are many circumstances in which cruise missiles will not be the weapon of choice. For example, a manned aircraft can mount many combat sorties, whereas a cruise missile is used only once. If aircraft attrition rates are low, as was the case during the 1991 Persian Gulf War, manned aircraft become extremely cost-effective when compared with a cruise missile. When loss rates are high, however, the difference is significantly reduced. Similarly, ballistic missiles may have an advantage over cruise missiles in circumstances requiring quick reaction. Thus, if the enemy target could move from the location at which it was detected, a supersonic ballistic missile would be preferable to a subsonic cruise missile.

11. "Tomahawk War Effectiveness Reduces A-X Stealth Requirement," *Aerospace Daily*, April 15, 1991, p. 85, cites a CEP of 20 feet.

12. The question of missile accuracy is discussed in Carus, *Ballistic Missiles*, 32–34, and Nolan, *Trappings of Power*, 70–72.

13. There is an important caveat to this statement. It will be possible to enhance the accuracy of ballistic missiles using satellite navigation systems. This could permit significant improvements in the accuracy of ballistic missiles that depend on inaccurate inertial guidance systems, such as the Soviet Scud-B. But this will only compensate for errors that appear during the boost phase, and as a result the improvements will be less than those possible with cruise missiles. Semiballistic missiles, which can maneuver during the entire flight of the missile, might be able to attain accuracies comparable to those achievable with cruise missiles. It is unclear whether satellite navigation systems can be employed to enhance the accuracy of guided reentry vehicles, such as those used on the Pershing II missile.

14. Kenneth P. Werrell, *The Evolution of the Cruise Missile*

(Maxwell Air Force Base, Alabama: Air University Press, 1985), 61.

15. Norman Friedman, *World Naval Weapons Systems* (Annapolis: U.S. Naval Institute Press, 1989), 70.

16. Stanley W. Kandero, "Tomahawk Missile Excels in First Wartime Use," *Aviation Week and Space Technology*, January 21, 1991, p. 61.

17. Kosta Tsipis, "Cruise Missiles," *Scientific American*, February 1977, p. 24.

18. Steven J. Zaloga, *Soviet Air Defense Missiles* (Alexandria, Va.: Jane's Information Group, 1989), 231.

19. Doug Richardson, *Stealth* (New York: Orion Books, 1989), 150, 154.

20. Lt. Col. V. Chumak, "Cruise Missiles and Combat against Them," *Vestnik Protivovozdushnyy Oborony* (Russian), December 1988, pp. 78–80, as translated in Joint Publications Research Service (JPRS), *Soviet Union: Military Affairs*, February 22, 1989, p. 41.

21. Friedman, *World Naval Weapons Systems*, 70.

22. Pierre Langereux, "France's ASMP Nuclear Cruise Missile Operational," *Military Technology*, July 1986, p. 67.

23. Bill Sweetman, *Stealth Bomber* (Osceola, Wis.: Motorbooks International, 1989), 48.

24. This paragraph is drawn from Toomay, "Technical Characteristics," 34–35.

25. "Turbojet Updates China's C 801," *Jane's Defence Weekly*, February 25, 1989, p. 321; Friedman, *World Naval Weapons Systems*, 79–80.

26. Reed, "Matra Plans New Cruise Missile."

27. James C. Hyde, "Block III Tomahawk: Coming This Summer to an Air Theater Near You?" *Armed Forces Journal International*, June 1991, p. 24.

28. Ibid.

29. The United States, Soviet Union, France, Great Britain, Japan, Sweden, Israel, China, Germany, and Taiwan are all believed to have developed air-launched cruise missiles.

30. Berend Derk Bruins, "U.S. Naval Bombardment Missiles, 1940–1958: A Study of the Weapons Innovation Process" (Ph.D. diss., Columbia University, 1981), 204.

31. The United States developed a delivery system for chemical and biological agents using unmanned aircraft. These are men-

tioned in U.S. Army Material Command, *Engineering Design Handbook – Elements of Terminal Ballistics, Part One: Introduction, Kill Mechanisms and Vulnerability (U)*, AMC Pamphlet AMC 706-160, NTIS AD 389 219, November 1962. For a discussion of biological and chemical munitions, see Stockholm International Peace Research Institute [SIPRI], *The Problem of Chemical and Biological Warfare*, vol. 2 (New York: Humanities Press, 1973), 72–81.

32. There are conflicting figures for the number of TLAM launches during the war. The one given here came from U.S. Department of Defense, *Conduct of the Persian Gulf Conflict: An Interim Report to Congress*, July 1991, pp. 6–8. Other figures have appeared in the press. For example, "Navy Dropped 11 Million Pounds of Bombs during 31 Days in Iraq War," *Aerospace Daily*, March 13, 1991, p. 428B, claims that 264 TLAM-C, 27 TLAM-D, and 7 SLAM land attack cruse missiles were expended during the war. "Tomahawk War Effectiveness Reduces A-X Stealth Requirement" states that 284 TLAMs were used, 90 percent TLAM-C and 10 percent TLAM-D.

33. "SLAMs Hit Iraqi Target in First Combat Firing," *Aviation Week and Space Technology*, January 28, 1991, pp. 31–32. According to the press report, the U.S. Air Force may have conventionally armed versions of the ALCM, although originally the missile was built only as a nuclear-armed weapon. The story also claims that the U.S. Air Force had a new type of missile and that this "black" weapon was used in the attacks. See "Conventional ALCMs, Black LRCSW/MSOW Replacement Strike Iraq," *Aerospace Daily*, February 6, 1991, p. 207.

34. U.S. Department of Defense, *Conduct of the Persian Gulf Conflict*.

35. Ibid. The number of TLAMs carried on a ship varies considerably. There are even substantial differences within classes. The battleships are equipped with 8 launchers, each with 4 missiles, for a total of 32 Tomahawks per ship. Some Spruance class destroyers have two-quad box launchers, whereas others have vertical launchers carrying up to 61 missiles. Most Ticonderoga-class guided missile cruisers have two 61-cell vertical launchers, but the launchers carry a variable mix of Standard SM-2 surface-to-air missiles and Tomahawks. Most Los Angeles class attack submarines are equipped with 12 vertical Tomahawk launch tubes. See A. D. Baker III, *Combat Fleets of the World,*

1990/1991: Their Ships, Aircraft, and Armaments, Bernard Preze-lin, ed. (Annapolis: U.S. Naval Institute Press, 1990), 777–802.

36. U.S. Department of Defense, *Conduct of the Persian Gulf Conflict*; "Tomahawk War Effectiveness Reduces A-X Stealth Requirement." Press reports claim that at least one of the missiles used in the first wave of launches failed to eject from the launch tube. See Thomas O'Toole, "Tomahawk Makes Its Wartime Debut," *Aerospace America*, March 1991, p. 12. "High Tech Weapons Give Quick Advantage in Mass Air Raid on Iraq," *Aerospace Daily*, January 18, 1991, p. 97, claims that the first salvo consisted of 52 missiles but one failed to launch.

37. "U.S. Draws Heavily on Inventory of Tomahawk Cruise Missiles," *Aerospace Daily*, January 21, 1991, p. 108. According to this source, only 51 missiles were launched and 50 were successful. "High Tech Weapons Give Quick Advantage," however, claims that the first salvo consisted of 52 missiles but one failed to launch.

38. "High Tech Weapons Give Quick Advantage."

39. "Navy Dropped 11 Million Pounds of Bombs."

40. Stanley W. Kandero, "U.S. Fires over 25% of Its Conventional Land Attack Tomahawks in First Week of War," *Aviation Week and Space Technology*, January 28, 1991, p. 29; "Tomahawk War Effectiveness Reduces A-X Stealth Requirement."

41. U.S. Department of Defense, *Conduct of the Persian Gulf Conflict* (quotation); "Tomahawk War Effectiveness Reduces A-X Stealth Requirement"; Robert Burns, "War Serves as Laboratory for Newest Sophisticated Weaponry," *Associated Press*, January 18, 1991, AM cycle. All Associated Press (AP) and United Press International (UPI) wire service reports cited in this study were taken from on-line databases.

42. "Tomahawk War Effectiveness Reduces A-X Stealth Requirement." Jack Reed, "Aerial Bombardment Hailed as 'Textbook' Operation," UPI, January 17, 1991, cites a BBC report claiming the attacks destroyed the headquarters building.

43. "Tomahawk War Effectiveness Reduces A-X Stealth Requirement."

44. Some of the damage to civilian targets attributed by the Iraqis to cruise missiles could have resulted from the impact of Iraqi-fired surface-to-air missiles that failed to self-destruct. It is also possible that in some instances misdirected laser-guided bombs dropped by F-117A fighters could have been responsible.

Chapter 3

1. According to the U.S. interpretation of the MTCR, missiles capable of exceeding the thresholds are banned even if the specific configuration does not violate the permitted levels. Thus, if a missile has a range of 200 kilometers carrying a 1,000-kilogram warhead, but its range can be extended to 400 kilometers by cutting the payload in half, the United States argues that it is prohibited by the agreement. See Speier, "The Missile Technology Control Regime," 116–117. Given the ease with which it is possible to extend the range of the Apache and similar turbojet-powered missiles, it is evident that the United States would oppose efforts to export them.

2. Abraham Rabinovich, *The Boats of Cherbourg* (New York: Seaver Books, Henry Holt and Company, 1988), provides the best history of the Gabriel.

3. Friedman, *World Naval Weapons Systems*, 83.

4. The original source documents for Operation Flower were among two sets of documents published by the Islamic Republic of Iran following the revolution that overthrew the shah. Details appear in minutes of meetings held during a trip to Israel by General H. Toufanian, Iranian minister of defense, in July 1977. Additional information came from documents produced during a trip to Iran by the commander of the Israeli Navy in July 1978.

5. The first press account to appear on the Flower was Martin Bailey, "The Blooming of Operation Flower," *The Observer*, February 2, 1986, p. 19. According to Bailey, the objective of the Flower program was a nuclear-armed missile. A close reading of the Iranian documents does not support his conclusions, however. Although the documents are sometimes ambiguous, they suggest that the Flower was in reality an antiship missile comparable to the U.S. Harpoon. General Ezer Weizman, Israel's defense minister at the time, was quoted as saying: "And on the next stage of the Harpoon, what we call the Flower." General Toufanian, Iran's defense minister, added comments indicating that the missile was a tactical weapon and that target acquisition and identification systems were critical to its performance, hardly necessary in a nuclear weapon. Moreover, it is evident that Israel did not perceive the program to be critical. General Weizman stated: "I am having a discussion with our Navy, and I am not sure that for our immediate future we need the 200 km. missile." Subsequently, he

noted: "If I have to decide on priorities, to me the 200 km. missile, the Flower, is not a top priority. The question is what are you and we going to do in 5, 6, 7 or 8 years when the Harpoon will become an older weapon." The only indication that the weapon might have a nuclear capability was in a comment by General Moshe Dayan, then Israel's minister of foreign affairs, who "raised the problem of the Americans' sensitivity to the introduction of the kind of missile envisaged in the joint project. He added that the ground-to-ground missile that is part of the joint project can be regarded also as a missile with a nuclear [war]head, because with a [war]head of 750 kg., it can be a double purpose one. General Dayan remarked that at some stage this problem will have to be raised with the Americans." The simplest interpretation of this statement is that Israel was worried that the United States would see the Flower as a nuclear weapon. It certainly does not support the interpretation that it was such a weapon. Significantly, Israel subsequently purchased submarine-launched versions of the U.S. Harpoon missile.

6. Friedman, *World Naval Weapons Systems*, 83. See also "FAC Missiles," *Navy International*, March 1989, p. 120.

7. *Sunday Times* (Johannesburg, South Africa), July 20, 1986.

8. Johannesburg *SAPA* (English), April 12, 1989, as reported in Foreign Broadcast Information Service (FBIS), *Daily Report: Sub-Saharan Africa*, April 17, 1989, p. 10.

9. Friedman, *World Naval Weapons Systems*, 88; "Hsiung Feng II a Major Boost for Taiwan," *Jane's Defence Weekly*, October 29, 1988, p. 1045. Taiwanese officials claim that the missile "is at the technological level of the Harpoon." Like most sources, it places the range at "more than 80 kilometers," but *International Defense Review*, October 1989, p. 1296, claims that the true figure is 180 kilometers.

10. Barbara Amouyal, "Taiwan Aims for Military Self Sufficiency by 2000," *Defense News*, October 15, 1990, p. 82 (quotation); "Latest Developments in Taiwan's Defence," *Military Technology*, April 1988, p. 78.

11. Joseph S. Bermudez, Jr., "North Korea's HY-2 'Silkworm' Programme," *Jane's Soviet Intelligence Review*, May 1989, pp. 203–207.

12. Christopher F. Foss, *Jane's Armour and Artillery, 1989–90*, 10th ed. (Alexandria, Va.: Jane's Information Group, 1989), p. 728.

13. Ibid., 724–725.

14. Christopher Foss, "Brazil Set to Enter Missile Market," *Jane's Defence Weekly*, February 7, 1987, p. 200.

15. According to the Indian Ministry of Defense, a "mobile missile coastal battery" has just been created at Coast Battery, Worli, at Bombay. Article by K. Subrahmanyam in *The Times of India* (English), May 8, 1989, p. 12, as given in JPRS, *Near East and South Asia*, July 10, 1989, p. 41, and Pushpinder Singh, "India Reviews Defence Needs," *Jane's Defence Weekly*, July 15, 1989, p. 89. It is not known, however, if this battery was armed with a Soviet-supplied missile like the SSC-3 (the shore-launched version of the SS-N-2 Styx), or if it was to be armed with a new Indian-made antiship missile. There are no reports of a Soviet sale of SSC-3 missiles to India. See Steven J. Zaloga, "Soviet Coastal Defence Missiles," *Jane's Soviet Intelligence Review*, April 1989, p. 172. See also Pushpinder Singh, "India's Agni Success Poses New Problems," *Jane's Defence Weekly*, June 3, 1989, p. 1053.

16. "Hong Kong *AFP*" (English), May 26, 1989, as reported in FBIS, *Daily Report: Near East and South Asia*, May 30, 1989, p. 60. It should be noted that Indian officials initially described the Agni intermediate-range ballistic missile as a "long-range surface-to-air missile." James Bruce, "India Ready to Test-fire Its Own Long-Range SAM," *Jane's Defence Weekly*, May 23, 1986, p. 1004.

17. Hormuz P. Mama, "Progress on India's New Tactical Missiles," *International Defence Review*, July 1989, p. 964. According to Mama, the propellant is magnesium-based, the case for the booster motor is made of maraging steel, and the case for the sustainer ramjet is of titanium alloy. This source provides a picture of the Akash, showing three missiles similar to the SA-6 mounted on a tracked launcher. Another source claims that it is the Trishul surface-to-air missile that is similar to the SA-6. See Singh, "India's Agni Success Poses New Problems." This is apparently confusion by the author—the Trishul has a range of only 10 kilometers, whereas the SA-6 has a range of 30 kilometers. The first tests of the Akash were scheduled for December 1989. The Akash is not expected to enter service until 1993. "Hong Kong *AFP*," May 26, 1989, pp. 60–61.

18. Shuey et al., "Missile Proliferation," 81.

19. Assistant Professor Kim Chol-hwan, doctor of engineering at the National Defense College, advocated developing a 400

kilometer-range ship-to-ship missile in an article published in *Kukpang Kwa Kisul*, January 1989, pp. 52–65, translated from the Korean in FBIS, *Daily Report: East Asia*, March 23, 1989, p. 39.

20. According to one account, Israeli intelligence was aware of all the Soviet equipment provided to Arab countries prior to the 1973 Arab-Israeli War with two exceptions. One of them was a Soviet 180-millimeter field artillery piece, and the other was the antiradiation version of the AS-5. See Zeev Schiff, *October Earthquake: Yom Kippur 1973*, trans. Louis Williams (Tel Aviv: University Publishing Projects, 1974), 159.

21. Duncan Lennox, "Stand-off Delivery Comes of Age," *Jane's Defence Weekly*, March 16, 1991, pp. 390–391. The author asserts that the missile was first shown in 1988, but this appears to be wrong. It is more likely to have been at the May 1989 Baghdad arms show.

22. Duncan Campbell, "Iraqi Missile Plan Linked to British Firms," *Independent* (London), November 4, 1990, p. 3; Alan George, "UK Foils Iraqi Cruise Missile," *Flight International*, October 2, 1990, p. 4.

23. "Iranian RPVs," *International Defense Review*, June 1989, p. 857. According to this report, Iran has three RPVs: the Baz, the Shahin, and an unidentified third system. They are radio-controlled, prop-driven, and currently configured to carry film cameras for reconnaissance missions.

24. Friedman, *World Naval Weapons Systems*, 83, 88.

25. Kenneth Munson, *World Unmanned Aircraft* (New York: Jane's Publishing, 1988), 54; "India Develops Its Own Cruise Missile," *New Scientist*, August 4, 1983.

26. Robert Salvy and Gowri Sundaram, "Oriental Industry Comes of Age," *International Defense Review*, March 1990, p. 245.

27. Robert Salvy, "Unmanned Aerial Vehicles, Part 1: European Programs – France," *International Defense Review*, April 1989, pp. 453–456. The Mirach 100 is powered by a 52-kilogram-thrust Microturbo TRS18 turbojet.

28. Barbara Amouyal, "Israeli Weapon Expected to Be Cleared by DoD for Evaluation Testing," *Defense News*, July 10, 1989, p. 26.

29. The first description of the Delilah appeared in Edwin S. Townsley and Clarence A. Robinson, "Critical Technology Assessment in Israel and NATO Nations," Institute for Defense Analy-

ses, IDA Memorandum Report M-317, April 1987, p. III-56. A more detailed description is provided in an undated marketing brochure, "Delilah Unmanned Air Vehicle Decoy," published by Israel Military Industries.

30. Leonard S. Spector with Jacqueline R. Smith, *Nuclear Ambitions: The Spread of Nuclear Weapons, 1989-1990* (Boulder, Colo.: Westview Press, 1990), provides a detailed survey of nuclear proliferation. For an updated assessment, see Bill Gertz, "Israel, Pakistan, India Have Nuclear Bombs, Experts Say," *Washington Times*, June 20, 1991, p. A6. Citing a newly completed special national intelligence estimate, Gertz reports that Israel, Pakistan, and India have nuclear weapons and that Algeria, Iran, and Iraq have nuclear programs.

31. Statement of Rear Admiral Thomas A. Brooks before the U.S. House, Subcommittee on Seapower, Strategic, and Critical Materials, p. 57 (quotation); W. Seth Carus and Joseph S. Bermudez, Jr., "The North Korean 'Scud-B' Programme," *Jane's Soviet Intelligence Review*, April 1989, pp. 177–181; W. Seth Carus, "Chemical Warfare in the Middle East," *Policy Focus*, Washington Institute for Near East Policy, Research Memorandum No. 9, December 1988.

32. These issues are discussed in W. Seth Carus, *The Poor Man's Atomic Bomb? Biological Weapons in the Middle East*, Policy Paper No. 23 (Washington, D.C.: Washington Institute for Near East Policy, 1991), pp. 57–64.

33. "Missiles in the Middle East: A New Threat to Stability," *Policy Focus*, Washington Institute for Near East Policy, Research Memorandum No. 6, June 1988.

34. See Carus, *Ballistic Missiles*, 6–7.

Chapter 4

1. Ironically, solving the demanding requirements of cruise missile guidance contributed to the development of the navigation systems for other types of weapons, including ballistic missiles. Donald Mackenzie, *Inventing Accuracy* (Boston: Massachusetts Institute of Technology, 1990), pp. 140–141, reports that the inertial navigation system used on the first Polaris ballistic missile submarines, the Ships Inertial Navigation System, was an

adaptation of the XN-6 guidance package originally developed by the Autonetics Division of North American Aviation for use in the Navaho intercontinental cruise missile.

2. Tsipis, "Cruise Missiles," 24.

3. Werrell, *Evolution of the Cruise Missile*, 135.

4. David Hughes, "Northrop Develops Miniature Laser Gyros for Tactical Missiles," *Aviation Week and Space Technology*, February 8, 1988, pp. 77–78.

5. Hormuz P. Mama and Stephane Chenard, "India's Mixed Bag of Launchers," *Space Markets*, April 1989, p. 258 (comments on gyroscopes).

6. Werrell, *Evolution of the Cruise Missile*, 110–111.

7. Ibid., 136–139.

8. Nick Cook, "SPARTAN Is Key to GR1 Update," *Jane's Defence Weekly*, May 25, 1991, p. 885.

9. "French Apache MSOW Takes Another Step Forward," *International Defense Review*, October 1989, p. 1300; Cook, "Saab Seeks ASOM Missile Partner"; Gunston, *Encyclopedia of Aircraft Armament*, p. 111.

10. "An Embargo Cannot Throttle Us – Dr. Abdul Kalam," *Frontline*, June 10–23, 1989, p. 11; "Emphasis Was on Re-entry Technology," *Frontline*, June 10–23, 1989, p. 15.

11. Xi Information Processing Systems, an Israeli company, distributes promotional literature describing a number of products that rely on digital mapping techniques. For example, its Pathmarker system uses digital maps for the flight planning and mission control of tactical mini-RPVs. Some of the company's mapping systems are designed for use on personal computers, such as the IBM PC/AT.

12. Toomay, "Technical Characteristics," 38–39.

13. An excellent explanation of GPS is given in Jeff Hurn, *GPS: A Guide to the Next Utility* (Sunnyvale, Calif.: Trimble Navigation, 1989).

14. Bruce D. Nordwall, "GPS Applications, Production Grow as System Gains Acceptance," *Aviation Week and Space Technology*, October 31, 1988, pp. 83, 85.

15. Philip J. Klass, "Soviets' Release of Glonass Data Will Ease Acceptance of Navsats," *Aviation Week and Space Technology*, June 6, 1988, p. 45; Stephane Chenard, "GLONASS Twin to GPS?" *Space Markets*, March 1989, pp. 170–175.

16. Philip J. Klass, "Industry Devising GPS Receivers with Hybrid Navigation Aids," *Aviation Week and Space Technology*, December 14, 1987, pp. 121–123.

17. Philip J. Klass, "First Production GPS Receiver Delivered Ahead of Schedule," *Aviation Week and Space Technology*, September 21, 1987, pp. 93–101.

18. "Rockwell Produces World's Smallest 5-Channel Global Positioning System Receiver," *Aviation Week and Space Technology*, April 15, 1991, p. 48.

19. Bruce D. Nordwall, "Civilian GPS Users Fear Pentagon's Ability to Degrade System Accuracy," *Aviation Week and Space Technology*, October 14, 1988, p. 71.

20. Bruce W. Henderson, "DARPA Contract Boosts FOG/ Global Positioning System," *Aviation Week and Space Technology*, January 14, 1991, pp. 42–43; "DARPA to Merge GPS, Inertial Guidance into Small, Accurate Guidance Systems," *Aviation Week and Space Technology*, February 25, 1991, p. 58.

21. Author telephone interview with Stephen Colwell of the Global Positioning Satellite Association, July 24, 1991.

22. Nordwall, "GPS Applications," 83, 85.

23. For a discussion of the difference, see J. F. Roeber, "Accuracy: What Is It? Why Do I Need It? How Much Do I Need?" *Navigation*, Summer 1983, pp. 171–178.

24. Vincent Kiernan, "Civilian Users Hampered by Federal GPS Policy," *Space News*, December 10–16, 1990, pp. 3, 21.

25. See Vincent Kiernan and Renee Saunders, "Pentagon Limits Accuracy of Navstar Data for Civilian Use" (editorial), *Defense News*, July 8, 1991, p. 21.

26. Rudolph M. Kalafus, "Differential GPS Standards," *Sea Technology*, March 1985, pp. 52–54.

27. Walter F. Blanchard, "DGPS via INMARSAT," *Proceedings of ION GPS-90, Third International Technical Meeting of the Satellite Division of the Institute of Navigation*, Institute of Navigation, Washington, D.C., September 19–21, 1990, p. 244.

28. Nordwall, "GPS Applications," 85. Author telephone interview with Stephen Colwell. George Zachmann, "GPS Accuracy for Civil Marine Navigation," *Sea Technology*, March 1989, p. 11, claims that it should be possible to obtain accuracies of 3 to 5 meters using differential GPS at ranges of 200 to 500 kilometers from the differential transmitter.

29. Efforts to enhance GPS accuracy for civil aviation appli-

cations are described in Philip J. Klass, "Integrated GPS/MLS System Could Be Useful for Terminal Area Operations," *Aviation Week and Space Technology*, February 18, 1991, pp. 56–57, and Edward H. Phillips, "GPS/ITU Data Guides New Autoland System," *Aviation Week and Space Technology*, January 7, 1991, p. 56.

30. Klass, "Soviets' Release of Glonass Data"; Philip J. Klass, "Pentagon Urged to Confirm Policy Allowing Civilian Use of GPS Navsats," *Aviation Week and Space Technology*, January 8, 1990, pp. 57–58; Raymond A. Eastwood, "East Meets West – Integrating GPS and GLONASS," *Sea Technology*, March 1990, pp. 10–14.

31. Philip J. Klass, "Inmarsat's GPS Proposal to Undergo Evaluation," *Aviation Week and Space Technology*, May 19, 1990, p. 103; Carole A. Shifrin, "Inmarsat Selects Designer-Builder for Four New, Highly Flexible Satellites," *Aviation Week and Space Technology*, December 10, 1990, p. 64.

32. Philip J. Klass, "Inmarsat Decision Pushes GPS to Forefront of Civil Nav-Sat Field," *Aviation Week and Space Technology*, January 14, 1991, p. 34.

33. Edward R. Slack, "Towards a Global Differential Service," *Proceedings of ION GPS-90*, p. 323.

34. Kiernan and Saunders, "Pentagon Limits Accuracy."

35. Author telephone interview with Stephen Colwell.

36. Rupert Pengelley, "New UAV System Developments from Israel," *International Defense Review*, September 1989, p. 1238; "Delilah Unmanned Air Vehicle Decoy," undated sales brochure produced by Israel Military Industry (quotation); "Targeting F-5Es for Retrofit," *Jane's Defence Weekly*, May 19, 1990, p. 965.

37. *Armed Forces* (Johannesburg), July 1989, p. 13, as reported in FBIS, *Daily Report: Sub-Saharan Africa*, September 8, 1989, p. 34; "An Embargo Cannot Throttle Us."

38. Michael A. Dornheim, "Egypt Begins Using Unmanned Aircraft for Reconnaissance," *Aviation Week and Space Technology*, January 23, 1989, p. 57.

39. The United States is developing inertially aided munitions (IAMs), which will be guided by glide bombs using an inexpensive inertial navigation system to provide guidance instructions. Preliminary tests suggest that it is possible to attain accuracies of less than 10 meters using IAMs. It is estimated that an IAM add-on package would cost about $15,000 per bomb.

Barbara Opall, "AF Mulls Low-Cost, Smart Modification to Dumb Gravity Bombs," *Defense News*, February 4, 1991, p. 38.

40. "Late 1988 Delivery Date Set for Harpoon Land Attack Derivative," *Aviation Week and Space Technology*, January 18, 1988, p. 45.

41. Toomay, "Technical Characteristics," p. 39, citing an article in *Aviation Week and Space Technology*; "French Apache MSOW Takes Another Step Forward."

42. "An Embargo Cannot Throttle Us"; "Emphasis Was on Re-entry Technology."

43. The Popeye is known in the United States as the AGM-142 Have Nap. It will be used on B-52 bombers. According to Bill Sweetman, "United States: B-2 Spearheads Bomber Modernisation," *International Defense Review*, August 1989, p. 1039, it is "a highly accurate, electro-optically guided missile with a 320 kg. warhead and a 90 km.-range." The entire weapon weighs 3,000 pounds (1,400 kilograms) and has a television system suitable for daylight use only. See *International Defense Review*, August 1989, p. 1068. Given the technologies involved, the Popeye should be reasonably expensive, probably costing between $500,000 and $1 million per weapon.

The Opher is produced by Elbit. It consists of the infrared seeker (which is contained in a stabilized housing), the guidance computer, and control surfaces. Kits are available for 500-pound Mk. 82 and 1,000-pound Mk. 83 bombs, but versions for larger bombs are under development. The first kits were delivered in late 1988. The Opher costs $35,000. See "A Far Cry from the Iron Bomb: Recent Developments in Air-to-Ground Munitions," *Armada International*, April 1988, pp. 32–34; *International Defense Review*, November 1989, p. 1581.

The Pyramid was developed by Rafael. It is described as a "low cost system," but no price is available. The Pyramid is intended for circumstances where it is necessary to attack heavily defended, high-priority targets, such as ships, buildings, and surface-to-air missile batteries. Video images are transmitted to the launching aircraft through a data link. Once a target is selected, the video image is locked onto the target. It can be used only during daylight. See "A Far Cry from the Iron Bomb," 34; *International Defense Review*, December 1987, p. 1680; *IDF Journal*, Winter 1989, p. 47.

44. Guy Willis, "Open Sesame! Baghdad Show Reveals Iraqi

Military-Industrial Capabilities," *International Defense Review*, June 1989, p. 838; "Rocket Projects Continue," *Jane's Defence Weekly*, May 20, 1989, p. 926.

    45. "Rocket Projects Continue"; Willis, "Open Sesame!"

Chapter 5

    1. An example of the potential difficulties involved in the integration of cruise missiles is the Pave Tiger. The Pave Tiger was a so-called kamikaze drone funded by the U.S. Air Force to attack ground-based electronic jamming systems. The program was cancelled when costs escalated because of integration problems. See Bill Sweetman, "Unmanned Air Vehicles Make a Comeback," *International Defense Review*, November 1985, p. 1775.

    2. All of these countries are mentioned in Munson, *World Unmanned Aircraft*, except for Iran, Iraq, and South Korea. It is unclear if Saudi Arabia ought to be included. According to Munson (p. 68), Saudi Arabia produces the MCS PL-60 mini-RPV. This system was originally developed and produced in the United States. Production of the mini-RPV was moved to Saudi Arabia about 1979, but Munson is uncertain if any were actually built after the transfer.

    Recent information on two new Indian mini-RPVs is given in Salvy and Sundaram, "Oriental Industry Comes of Age." The most recent of the mini-RPVs will be capable of carrying a payload of 45 kilograms. Iranian production of RPVs is discussed in Dan Boyle and Robert Salvy, "Iranian RPVs," *International Defense Review*, June 1989, p. 857. Iraq's activities are covered in Willis, "Open Sesame!"

    At least three companies in South Korea are working on RPVs or drones. Samsung's Aerospace Research and Development Center was involved in design studies for RPVs. "Samsung Keys Future Growth to FX Fighter Program," *Aviation Week and Space Technology*, June 12, 1989, p. 217. The Daewoo company was designing a large, long-endurance reconnaissance RPV made out of composite materials, according to "Daewoo Expands Machining Base to Increase Production Capacity," *Aviation Week and Space Technology*, June 12, 1989, p. 223. Another company, Korean Air, license-built copies of the Northrop KD2R-5 prop-driven target drone. See "Korean Air Negotiates Agreement to

Coproduce UH-60," *Aviation Week and Space Technology*, June 12, 1989, p. 227.

3. Munson, *World Unmanned Aircraft*, 12, 65. The Bigua is powered by a turbojet engine with a 115-kilogram thrust and can carry a payload of up to 70 kilograms. Its maximum range is 900 kilometers.

4. Munson, *World Unmanned Aircraft*, 65–66; Jeffrey M. Lenorovitz, "Italian RPV Wins $16-Million Bid for NATO Missile Range Service," *Aviation Week and Space Technology*, February 23, 1987, pp. 52–53; Robert Salvy, "The Italian Mirach Family of RPVs," *International Defense Review*, November 1985, p. 1785. The Mirach 600 is powered by two 378-kilogram thrust turbojet engines, possibly Microturbo TRI 60-2 engines of the type used on the Swedish RBS-15 ASCM.

5. Friedman, *World Naval Weapons Systems*, 87; Munson, *World Unmanned Aircraft*, 36, 76; "Reconnaissance Drones Developed to Meet Expanding Soviet Needs," *Jane's Defence Weekly*, August 10, 1985, pp. 260–261.

6. Munson, *World Unmanned Aircraft*, 54. The Iranians have displayed four different RPVs but have given no specifications for any of them. The three RPVs credited with a potential attack capability were the Baz, Shahin, and "22006." The mini-RPVs were on display at an Ankara arms show in May 1989. See Salvy, "Iranian RPVs," 857. Iran is known to have an additional, unnamed RPV, which appeared at an arms exhibition in Tehran in October 1988. See W. Seth Carus and Joseph S. Bermudez, "Show Throws Light on Iranian Arms Industry," *Jane's Defence Weekly*, November 19, 1988, p. 1253.

7. Statement of Rear Admiral William O. Studeman, U.S. Navy, Director of Naval Intelligence, before the U.S. House, Subcommittee on Seapower, Strategic, and Critical Materials, Armed Services Committee on Intelligence Issues, March 1, 1988, p. 52.

8. Statement of Rear Admiral Thomas A. Brooks, U.S. Navy, Director of Naval Intelligence, before the U.S. House, Subcommittee on Seapower, Strategic, and Critical Materials, pp. 56–57, 66.

9. Ibid., p. 67.

10. This is a partial list based on preliminary research:

• India: A short discussion of Indian use of composite materials in aircraft programs appears in Michael Howarth, Hormuz Mama, and Gowri Sundaram, "India: Indigenous Programs Flourish amid Defense Modernization," *International Defense Review*, April 1986, p. 444.

- Israel: The airframes of some of Israel's mini-RPVs are known to be built from composite materials. See Munson, *World Unmanned Aircraft*, 58–59, for a discussion of the Pioneer.

- South Africa: The Atlas Aircraft Corporation has displayed a prototype attack helicopter, the Puma XTP-1, which relies heavily on composite structures. See Helmoed-Roemer Heitman, "South Africa's Helicopter Program," *Military Technology*, July 1987, p. 51.

- South Korea: According to one report, a South Korean company is developing an RPV made of composite materials. See "Daewoo Expands Machining Base."

- Taiwan: It appears that Taiwan's new fighter will rely heavily on composite components. See "Ching-Kuo Prototype Unveiled," *International Defense Review*, January 1989, p. 14.

11. Amouyal, "Taiwan Aims for Military Self Sufficiency."

12. "Stealth in the Missile Market," *Jane's Defence Weekly*, April 13, 1991, p. 602; "ASLP Shapes Up," *Jane's Defence Weekly*, June 22, 1991, p. 1082.

13. Mark Hewish, "ASMs: Increased Accuracy at Lower Cost," *International Defense Review*, November 1990, pp. 1261–1263. The U.S. Navy has flown the Advanced Interdiction Weapon System (AIWS) to ranges of 30 kilometers. The AIWS – now undergoing testing – is expected to replace many of the existing laser-guided and television-guided weapons, such as the Paveway, Walleye, and Maverick. The AIWS will be fitted with an integrated GPS-inertial guidance package as well as an optical system for terminal guidance. See "Contest for AIWS Gets Underway," *Jane's Defence Weekly*, April 13, 1991, p. 584; "TI/LTV AIWS Flight Tests Successful," *Jane's Defence Weekly*, May 25, 1991, p. 885.

14. Carus, *Ballistic Missiles*, 23.

15. "International Gas Turbine Engines," *Aviation Week and Space Technology*, March 20, 1989, p. 181; Friedman, *World Naval Weapons Systems*, 88.

16. "International Gas Turbine Engines"; "Turbojet Updates China's C 801," *Jane's Defence Weekly*, February 25, 1989, p. 321.

17. This is a partial list of Third World countries producing turbojet engines suitable for use in combat aircraft:

• India: Although initial versions of the new LCA fighter will rely on U.S.-supplied F-404 engines, India is continuing to develop its own GTX engine. See Howarth, Mama, and Sundaram, "India."

• Israel: Currently produces the J79 jet engine, used in the F-4 Phantom and the Kfir. See John W. R. Taylor, ed., *Jane's All the World's Aircraft, 1987–88* (London: Jane's Publishing Company, 1987), 910.

• South Africa: "Mirage into Cheetah . . . by Way of Kfir," *Air International*, April 1989, p. 184, reports that South Africa's main aircraft manufacturer, Atlas, probably produces the French Atar 9K-50 fighter engine. In addition, according to Johannesburg *Sunday Times* (English), May 14, 1989, p. 2, as reported in FBIS, *Daily Report: Sub-Saharan Africa*, May 15, 1989, p. 9, Atlas is attempting to develop "state-of-the-art high performance jet engines" for the CAVA twin-engine multirole fighter aircraft now under design.

• Taiwan: "Ching-Kuo Prototype Unveiled" reports that a U.S. company, Garrett, has developed the TFE1042 engine for use by Taiwan in the Indigenous Defensive Fighter (IDF) now under development by the Aero Industry Development Center (AIDC).

18. An example of a country with a developing engine industry is South Korea, which currently is license-building the Allison 225 jet engine for use on helicopters. "Samsung Keys Future Growth to FX Fighter Program," *Aviation Week and Space Technology*, June 12, 1989, p. 217.

19. Munson, *World Unmanned Aircraft*, 54.

20. Taylor, *Jane's All the World's Aircraft*, 909–910. The engine weighs 67 kilograms, generates 368 kilograms of thrust, and has a specific fuel consumption of 1.22 kilograms of fuel per hour per kilogram of thrust.

21. Townsley and Robinson, "Critical Technology Assessment," III-54.

22. Johannesburg *SAPA* (English), April 12, 1989, as reported in FBIS, *Daily Report: Sub-Saharan Africa*, April 17, 1989, p. 10. The South Africans showed a model of the engine at an arms show in Chile in 1986. "The Armaments Corporation of South Africa at FIDA '86," *Military Technology*, July 1986, p. 115. According to this source, it is designed for "drones, targets, and remotely piloted vehicles." Significantly, the South Africans ac-

companied the engine with a photograph of what appears to be an ASCM. For another report of the engine, which essentially confirms these details, see *Sunday Times* (Johannesburg, South Africa), July 20, 1986, unpaged. The technical details of the engine are from Mark Lambert, "The Second World of Armaments: Chile and South Africa at FIDA '86," *International Defense Review*, May 1986, p. 493. This report suggests that the engine could be used for "anti-ship missiles, reconnaissance drones, and anti-armour attack." At that time, South Africa was testing "several prototypes."

It is possible that the APA-1 is the result of the "Apartment" project, which was recently mentioned in the South African press. Apparently, this project was started in the early 1980s and resulted in a "light weight jet engine" suitable for use in an RPV. The engine reportedly "operated successfully for hours, long in excess of the design specification." See "The Rooivalk XH-2 Combat Support Helicopter," *Armed Forces* (English), February 1990, p. 13, as reproduced in FBIS, *Daily Report: Sub-Saharan Africa*, March 7, 1990, p. 13.

23. Friedman, *World Naval Weapons Systems*, 88.

24. *Jane's All the World's Aircraft, 1985–86*, p. 786; *Defense Attache*, no. 1, 1986, p. 41.

25. It appears that this was the warhead originally built about 1960 for use in the AGM-12C Bullpup B missile developed for the U.S. Navy. See Gunston, *Encyclopedia of Aircraft Armament*, 120.

26. Hyde, "Block III Tomahawk."

27. This is probably only a partial list. Cluster munition warheads for artillery rockets and short-range ballistic missiles are widely manufactured in the Third World. Brazil (Astros II SS-40 and SS-60), Egypt (220-millimeter Sakr-80 and 122-millimeter Sakr-30), Iraq (550-millimeter Laith 90, 400-millimeter Ababil 100, 262-millimeter Ababil 50, and the Sajil 40 and 60), and Israel (MAR-290, MAR-350, and LAR-160) are reported to have such munitions. Foss, *Jane's Armour*, 724–725. The Indian short-range ballistic missile, the Prithvi, has a cluster munition warhead. See Carus, *Ballistic Missiles*, 36. Cluster munition aircraft bombs are being built in several Third World countries. Gunston, *Encyclopedia of Aircraft Armament*, 80–85, describes cluster bombs from Chile, Israel, and South Africa. India has started preproduction of an aircraft-delivered 270-kilogram cluster bomb with high-explo-

sive, incendiary, and HEAT bomblets. See Salvy and Sundaram, "Oriental Industry Comes of Age," 246. For data on Iraqi cluster bombs, see Willis, "Open Sesame!" South Korea produces 105-millimeter M444 armor-piercing improved conventional munition rounds, a cluster munition artillery shell. See John Gordon IV, "ROK Artillery – Present and Future," *Field Artillery*, February 1990, p. 14.

28. This description is based on sales literature distributed by Cardoen.

29. This is probably an incomplete list:

• Argentina: A fuel air explosive warhead is being developed for the Condor missile, apparently based on German technology. See Panorama, BBC Television Service (English), April 10, 1989, as reported in FBIS, *Daily Report: Western Europe*, April 11, 1989, pp. 4–5.

• India: On Indian development of fuel air explosives, see Howarth, Mama, and Sundaram, "India," 441; on Indian interest in such weapons for rockets, see Singh, "India's Agni Success Poses New Problems." See also Manoj Joshi, "Agni: Importance, Implications," *Frontline*, June 10–23, 1989, p. 8.

• Iraq: Willis, "Open Sesame!" In May 1989, Iraq claimed to have three "vacuum bombs," one displayed at the May Baghdad arms exposition and two other "more sophisticated types." See Baghdad *Al-Thawrah* (Arabic), April 28, 1989, pp. 3, 15, as translated in FBIS, *Daily Report: Near East and South Asia*, May 2, 1989, p. 21.

• Israel: A number of sources have claimed that Israel made use of a fuel air explosive in the 1982 Lebanon War. For one such report, see Col. I. Karenin, "Fuel Air Explosives," Moscow *Znamenosets* (Russian), December 31, 1988, p. 31, as translated in JPRS, *Soviet Military Affairs*, April 3, 1989, p. 42.

Chapter 6

1. See, for example, the Statement of Henry D. Sokolski, deputy for nonproliferation policy, Office of the Assistant Secretary of Defense, International Security Affairs, U.S. Department of Defense, before the U.S. Senate, Joint Economic Committee,

Subcommittee on Technology and National Security, April 23, 1991.

2. For a discussion of these issues from an Israeli perspective, see chapter 3 in Hirsh Goodman and W. Seth Carus, *The Future Battlefield and the Arab-Israeli Conflict* (New Brunswick, N.J.: Transaction Publishers, 1990). Specific systems of potential interest to Israel are listed on p. 67.

3. Although no Third World country can build a strategic bomber comparable to those produced by the United States or the former Soviet Union, this may not prevent some Third World countries from acquiring long-range strike capabilities. Use of aerial refueling could extend the range of long-range strike aircraft, but few Third World countries are likely to have the command and control and logistics infrastructures needed to conduct such operations. Alternatively, a large civilian transport aircraft could be converted into a bomber. The extent of the threat is unclear, however, and the whole subject deserves additional research.

4. Bond, "Intelligence Agencies See Weaker Warsaw Pact Threat."

5. Werrell, *Evolution of the Cruise Missile*, 82–97 and 113–119, recaps the history of these programs.

6. John Cushman, "7 Nations Agree to Limit Export of Big Rockets," *New York Times*, April 17, 1989, p. A1. See also Speier, "The Missile Technology Control Regime," 115–121; Nolan, *Trappings of Power*, 115–122, 145–155.

7. Author interview with French government official, July 3, 1991.

8. The documents associated with MTCR were reprinted in Trevor Findlay, ed., *Chemical Weapons & Missile Proliferation—With Implications for the Asia/Pacific Region* (Boulder, Colo.: Lynn Rienner Publishers, 1991), 149–161 (quotation at 157).

9. Statement of Ambassador Ronald F. Lehman II, director, Arms Control and Disarmament Agency, on Nuclear and Missile Proliferation, before the U.S. Senate Committee on Governmental Affairs, May 18, 1989. Interview data suggest that the country involved in these transactions was Taiwan, which was able to acquire Harpoon cruise missile technology.

10. Bruce A. Smith, "New Vehicles Mark Teledyne Ryan's Strong Return to RPV Business," *Aviation Week and Space Technology*, November 30, 1987, pp. 54–55.

11. Carol Reed, "Matra Plans New Cruise Missile."

12. Langereux, "France's ASMP Nuclear Cruise Missile Operational."

13. Office of the Press Secretary, The White House, "Fact Sheet on Middle East Arms Control Initiative," May 29, 1991, p. 2.

14. United Nations, General Assembly, *Establishment of a Nuclear-Weapon-Free Zone in the Region of the Middle East*, A/45/435, October 10, 1990, pp. 41–42. For additional expressions of support for a ban on surface-to-surface missiles in the Middle East, see "Middle East Arms Control: A Five Point Plan," *F.A.S. Public Interest Report*, March–April 1991, pp. 1–2, 6–8; Max M. Kampelman and Edward C. Luck, "Ban Missiles in the Middle East," *Washington Post*, April 18, 1991; and Ken Adelman, "Can Missile Pact Cool Mideast Fires?" *Washington Times*, June 12, 1991, p. G3.

15. Alan Riding, "Big 5 Pledge for Mideast: Ban Devastating Arms," *New York Times*, July 10, 1991, p. A9; text of the joint communiqué, "Meeting of the Five on Arms Transfers and Non-Proliferation (Paris, 6th and 9th of July 1991)," p. 2 (quotations).

16. Kathleen C. Bailey, "Can Missile Proliferation Be Reversed?" *Orbis*, Winter 1991, p. 13, calling for a global INF agreement, and Kathleen C. Bailey, "Arms Control for the Middle East," *International Defense Review*, April 1991, p. 311, advocating only a Middle East INF Treaty.

17. Article VII, Section 4, of the Treaty between the United States of America and the Union of Soviet Socialist Republics on the Elimination of Their Intermediate-Range and Shorter-Range Missiles.

18. Werrell, *Evolution of the Cruise Missile*, 41–61, summarizes the entire history of the V-1 and the campaign to defend against it.

19. A pulse jet is a relatively simple engine consisting of a tube with a shutter at the front. When the shutter is closed, fuel is injected into a combustion chamber and detonated. After the exhaust gases are forced out the rear of the engine, the shutter is opened, fresh air enters, the shutter is closed again, and the cycle is repeated. Despite the simplicity of the pulse jet, which made it relatively light and cheap to build, it was not fuel efficient. Toward the end of World War II, the Germans were planning to replace the pulse jet with a turbojet that would have tripled the

range of the missile. See Anthony L. Kay, *Buzz Bomb*, Monogram Close-up 4 (Boylston, Mass.: Monogram Aviation Publications, 1977), 1ff, 27.

20. Werrell, *Evolution of the Cruise Missile*, 50, 54, 58.

21. This assessment of defenses draws heavily on Gordon MacDonald, Jack Ruina, and Mark Balaschak, "Soviet Strategic Air Defense," *Cruise Missiles: Technology, Strategy, Politics*, Richard K. Betts, ed. (Washington, D.C.: Brookings Institution, 1981), 53–82, and on Lt. Col. V. Chumak, "Cruise Missiles and Combat against Them," as translated in JPRS, *Soviet Union: Military Affairs*, 40–42.

22. Rabinovich, *The Boats of Cherbourg*, 3–11, 303.

23. The following assessment is derived from Lt. Col. V. Chumak, "Cruise Missiles and Combat against Them," as transated in JPRS, *Soviet Union: Military Affairs*, 40.

24. Zaloga, *Soviet Air Defence Missiles*, 75, 231, 288.

25. Ibid., 110–117; International Institute for Strategic Studies, *The Military Balance, 1990–1991* (London: Brassey's, 1990), p. 47.

Appendix

1. Werrell, *Evolution of the Cruise Missile*, 136–139; Gary H. Anthes, "Missile Guidance," *Computerworld*, January 28, 1991, p. 90; "Tomahawk War Effectiveness Reduces A-X Stealth Requirement."

2. Robert Holzer, "Modified Sub Tomahawk Flies Farther in Gulf," *Defense News*, February 18, 1991, p. 37.

3. Stanley W. Kandero, "Evolving Cruise Missile Upgrades Stress Versatility, Flexibility," *Aviation Week and Space Technology*, November 23, 1987, p. 103.

4. Hyde, "Block III Tomahawk"; Kandero, "U.S. Fires over 25% of Its Conventional Land Attack Tomahawks," 29–30.

5. Kandero, "U.S. Fires over 25% of Its Conventional Land Attack Tomahawks," 30; Glenn W. Goodman, Jr., and Benjamin F. Schemmer, "Combat Upgrades: One Difference between Golf and War," *Armed Forces Journal International*, May 1991, p. 50. The performance of the new computer appears to be comparable to what could be achieved by a Third World country using commercial components. Such a computer could have greater processing

power than the new Tomahawk computer, yet it might be smaller and less expensive.

6. Floyd C. Painter, "U.S. Cruise Missiles Gird Strategic Objectives," *Defense Electronics*, November 1988, p. 38.

7. No official figures for the range of the ACM have been released. Some sources, such as Richardson, *Stealth*, 78–80, 150, estimate the range at 3,000 kilometers; others cite longer ranges. Painter, "U.S. Strategic Missiles Gird Strategic Defense," 41, for example, estimates 2,300 miles, or about 3,750 kilometers. Given that the ACM is considerably larger than the ALCM, yet carries a similar warhead, it seems likely that the new missile has a substantially longer range.

8. "Air Force to Present 1,000-Missile ACM Program to DAB," *Aerospace Daily*, April 12, 1991, p. 79B.

9. Unless otherwise noted, the following account is based on "SLAMs Hit Iraqi Target in First Combat Firing," *Aviation Week and Space Technology*, January 28, 1991, pp. 31–32; "Late 1988 Delivery Date Set for Harpoon Land Attack Derivative," *Aviation Week and Space Technology*, January 18, 1988, p. 45; and "Production-Model SLAM Scores Bull's-Eye in First Test Firing," *Aviation Week and Space Technology*, July 10, 1989, p. 30.

10. "Navy Dropped 11 Million Pounds of Bombs during 31 Days in Iraq War," *Aerospace Daily*, March 13, 1991, p. 428B.

11. "SLAMs Hit Iraqi Target in First Combat Firing."

12. Bill Sweetman, "TSSAM Unveiled as B-2 Match," *Jane's Defence Weekly*, June 15, 1991, p. 1009; Melissa Healy and Ralph Vartabedian, "Secret Work by Northrop on Missile Told," *Los Angeles Times*, June 7, 1991, pp. A1, A28; U.S. Department of Defense Regular Press Briefing, June 6, 1991, as transcribed by Federal News Service.

13. Sweetman, "TSSAM Unveiled as B-2 Match."

14. Richard Stevenson, "Northrop to Develop Army Antitank Missile," *New York Times*, June 21, 1991, p. D4. BAT will weigh about 20 kilograms and will be armed with a shaped charge warhead. By mid-1991, the BAT had been tested 30 times over a five-year period. See "Army Taps BAT as Top Antiarmor Munition," *Aviation Week and Space Technology*, July 15, 1991, p. 51.

15. Barbara Amouyal, "Air Force Planners Developing Hypersonic Missile for Future Fighter," *Defense News*, December 4, 1989, p. 34; Lennox, "Stand-off Delivery Comes of Age," 395.

16. Neil Munro, "Air Force, Navy Plan Next Generation of Long-Range Cruise Missiles," *Defense News*, September 18, 1989,

pp. 3, 81. Five contractors were selected to work on conceptual designs, and it was expected that in early 1991 at least two of the companies would be selected to complete the development of competing systems. See Len Famiglietti, "USA Begins Development of LRCSW," *Jane's Defence Weekly*, July 29, 1989, p. 153.

17. *Aerospace Daily*, February 6, 1991, p. 207.

18. Amouyal, "Israeli Weapon Expected to Be Cleared."

19. See "Reconnaissance and Combat Drones," *International Defense Review*, September 1987, pp. 1197–1198; "Air Force Narrows Competition for Tacit Rainbow Follow-On," May 23, 1988, p. 87; "Tacit Rainbow Endurance Questioned," *Flight International*, August 13, 1988. The Tacit Rainbows were expected to cost under $200,000 apiece. Amouyal, "Israeli Weapon Expected to Be Cleared."

20. Hewish, "ASMs: Increased Accuracy at Lower Cost," 1258. The SRAM-T is a tactical version of the SRAM II nuclear-armed missile used by the U.S. Strategic Air Command, and the SLAT is a version of a supersonic target drone.

21. Mark Hewish, "The Sea Eagle Anti-Ship Missile," *International Defense Review*, July 1987, pp. 937–939.

22. The following account is based on Langereux, "France's ASMP Nuclear Cruise Missile Operational," 62–71, and Christian Pochhacker, "Supersonic Cruise Missile," *International Combat Arms*, May 1987, pp. 56–57.

23. "French Apache MSOW Takes Another Step Forward." The missile will be composed of four components: a nose section containing the complete guidance package (80 kilograms), rear section containing the complete propulsion system (270 kilograms, including 95 kilograms of fuel), an upper section containing the wings and connections to the aircraft (110 kilograms), and the payload (740–770 kilograms). The payload will comprise more than 60 percent of the total weight of the missile. Because the system is modular in design, it should be possible to replace the propulsion section with one designed to provide longer ranges.

24. Carol Reed, "Matra Plans New Cruise Missile."

25. "Aerospatiale Nuclear-Armed Missile Designed for Speed, Radar Evasion," *Aviation Week and Space Technology*, June 24, 1991, p. 24; "ASLP Shapes Up," *Jane's Defence Weekly*, June 22, 1991, p. 1082.

26. Friedman, *World Naval Weapons Systems*, 66.

27. Sauerwein, "Unmanned Aerial Vehicles," 456–457.

28. Ibid., 456.

Index

168